About Teaching

4MAT® in the Classroom

by Bernice McCarthy

Illustrated by Margaret Gray Hudson

Published by About Learning, Incorporated

About Learning, Incorporated
Wauconda, IL
May, 2000

Art direction by Dennis McCarthy.
Book and cover design by Mary Fran Zidron.
Set in Cheltenham and Charlotte Sans type.
Printed by Mid-American Printing Systems, Inc.,
Chicago, IL.

ISBN: 1-929040-01-6

*4MAT and 4MATION are registered trademarks
of About Learning, Inc.*

This book is gratefully dedicated to
the best group of people one could ever work with–
the staff at About Learning, Incorporated.

–Bernice McCarthy

Table of Contents

*A child is a person who is going to carry on
what you have started.
He is going to sit where you are sitting,
and when you are gone, attend to those
things which you think are important…
the fate of humanity is in those hands.*

—Abraham Lincoln

About Teaching

This book is a revision of the original 4MAT book.

It explains in detail how to teach around the 4MAT cycle.

It will assist teachers who are learning to use and implement
The 4MAT System, a natural cycle of learning.

It contains many new insights and techniques on all eight steps of
this teaching model, and includes new sections on brain-compatible
teaching and learning.

May it be of help to those who want all learners to have
an equal chance.

Bonita Springs, Florida
Winter, 2000.

Introduction

Everything I have learned since 1979 when I set out to create a learning system that would work with all learners has led me back to the 4MAT cycle, the cycle that begins with meaning and ends with integrating new learning.

I have experienced the phenomenon of this cycle over and over again. No matter what the content, or who the learners, the elements of the cycle are in play. The cycle is natural; it describes how we learn.

It is how we come to know ourselves and others, act in relationships, ponder meaning, play with ideas, hypothesize, form solutions, master skills, adapt, and create. It is how humans find meaning.

Kurt Lewin[1] named it and David Kolb[2] brought it to the world's attention, and in 1979, I translated it into the language of instructional design with the first 4MAT book.

The cycle begins with experience, with our perceptions of what happens to us and how we feel about those experiences.

These perceptions lead to individualized images which we then form into cognitive and often visual conceptualizations. We rationalize what we see and act on our conclusions. This leads us to more complex understandings and further growth.

This is how humans come to meaning: experiencing their inner lives, perceiving the external world, conceptualizing that world, acting on those conceptualizations, and adapting and integrating those conceptualizations.

This process repeats with each new experience, as we enter into understanding and assimilate that knowing into what we are becoming.

Each learner's journey is unique. Teachers must create experiences that connect to their learners so they come to value the learning and adapt it to their own lives. This adaptive usefulness is the hallmark of all successful learning.

---

[1]Lewin, Kurt, 1951
[2]Kolb, David, 1983

Chapter One

The 4MAT Cycle

The Cycle is the Key

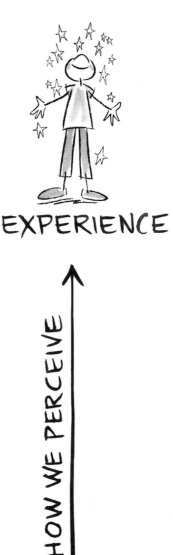

EXPERIENCE

HOW WE PERCEIVE

The cycle is a combination of two continua, the first, how we take in experience, and the second, how we act on what we take in.

It is the act of making meaning, the finest definition of learning I know.

Learning is the realization of something new and our response to that newness.

We perceive newness first with our senses, in direct experience. Learning invites us, presents itself. Then we move to the task of describing it, abstracting it, conceptualizing it.

Schools ask us to move to abstraction too quickly, before we've had a chance to feel what this new thing is about.

This first continuum is how we perceive: from direct experience to the cognitive task of abstracting that experience, conceptualizing it.

We generalize our experiences based on some connected schema from our past. Some of us are more fascinated with these experiences and how we feel about them, and so we linger there. Others hurry from the experience to the abstraction, more intrigued with objectifying what happens to them, more interested in fitting the newness into some form, not so intrigued by their subjective feelings about them. These preferences have a profound impact on how we learn.

ABSTRACTING

The movement along the Perceiving dimension from Direct Experience to Abstract Conceptualization is propelled by the processing dimension.

This processing continuum moves from reflection to action.

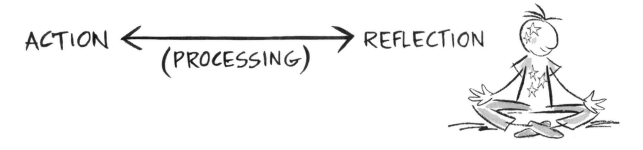

ACTION ←————— (PROCESSING) —————→ REFLECTION

We process our experiences by reflecting on them. This leads us to abstract those experiences, to create concepts about them, to generalize them.

For example, I meet a new person my first day on the job and am attracted by her, her attitude, the way she thinks, the energy she brings. Even though I have only a small amount of data, when I drive home that afternoon, I hunch there is the possibility of a rich friendship in the making. This is an example of how we place newness in perspective to our lives. This is the crucial place where we either accept or reject it. (Imagine how many students sit through content they have already dismissed!)

Through the act of reflecting on that person, I have moved from a direct experience of a person to the concept of "friend" and all that word implies for me. I have moved from perceiving her, to reflecting on her, to conceptualizing her by naming her with the words "possible friend," words that have rich, personal meaning for me.

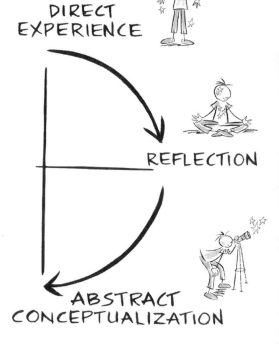

DIRECT EXPERIENCE

REFLECTION

ABSTRACT CONCEPTUALIZATION

The other end of the processing continuum is action.

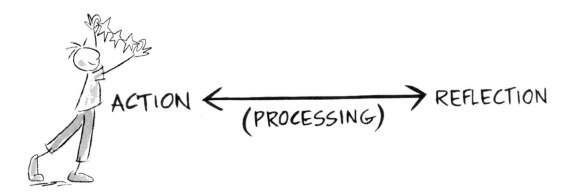

ACTION ←————— (PROCESSING) ————→ REFLECTION

I have moved from 12 o'clock to 6 o'clock on the cycle via reflective processing at 3 o'clock, from experience to concept, from feeling to classification and conceptualization (the notion of friend). But my learning is only half done.

Learning starts with **Me** at 12 o'clock, then moves to **It** at 6 o'clock as I name and classify. But in order to integrate the learning for myself, I must use it. And in the use of it, I return back to Me. Without that final return, nothing has been really learned.

I must act on my conceptualizations, try them out in the real world. I must move from the abstract back up to myself.
I must take action.

To return to the example of friend, I go to work over the next few weeks and spend time with my new colleague. I first chat with her, then share experiences and confide in her. I listen to her ideas, to her confidences. Over time, I come to enjoy our new friendship.

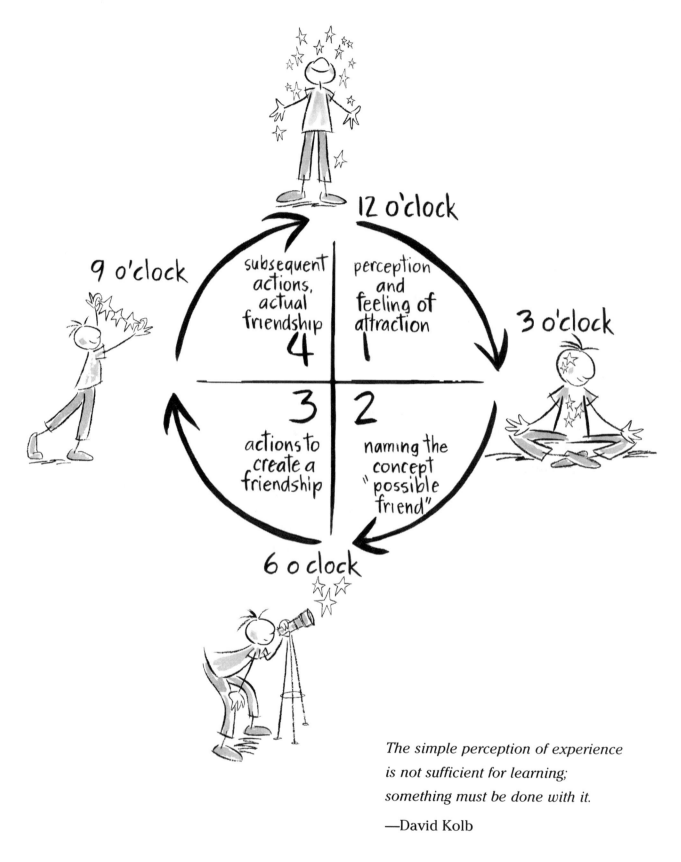

12 o'clock

9 o'clock

3 o'clock

6 o'clock

subsequent actions, actual friendship

4

perception and feeling of attraction

1

actions to create a friendship

3

2

naming the concept "possible friend"

The simple perception of experience is not sufficient for learning; something must be done with it.

—David Kolb

Chapter One: The 4MAT Cycle

I have moved from 6 o'clock, to my new acquaintance, back to 12 o'clock, where I have integrated this new learning. (In this case a person.)

I have integrated my meeting with a fellow colleague into a true friendship, a real change in my life.

I have made this final step by taking action (9 o'clock) which led me back to new experiences with friendship and relationship.

I have completed the cycle.

As with the perceiving dimension, learners have distinct preferences along the ends of the Processing continuum.

Some learners are more comfortable in Reflection. Others prefer Action.

These preferences have a profound impact on how people learn.

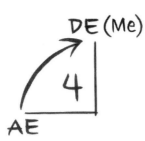

DE (Me)

4

AE

DE (Me)

1

RO

Putting It All Together

Learning moves from 12 o'clock, the sensory place, the "Me" place, where we feel our world, from direct experience (DE) into reflective observation (RO).

Then we assimilate the experience and abstract it into a concept (AC).

We stand back and examine, we name It. The 6 o'clock place is the "It" place, where things are objects to be examined and understood.

Then we try things out, finding out what personal meaning we can make of this experience, this thing, transforming concepts into actions via active experimentation (AE).

Lastly, we return to new direct experience (DE) with an ever-renewing focus. We have integrated meaning, concept, and action.

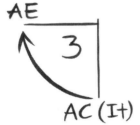

AE

3

AC (It)

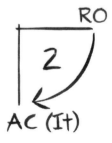

RO

2

AC (It)

Moving Around the Cycle

The movement around the 4MAT cycle represents the learning process itself.

It is a movement from experiencing,

> to reflecting,
>
> to conceptualizing,
>
> to tinkering and problem-solving,
>
> to integrating new learning with the self.

It is a movement that involves a constant balancing and rebalancing between being in experience and standing apart to analyze that experience,

> between subjective and objective,
>
> between connected and separate,
>
> between being and knowing.

From connectedness to separation, back to connectedness.
From "in here" to "out there."

First We Experience

EXPERIENCE

When we experience something new, we are initially immersed in it because when we are drawn to something, we approach it with our whole selves.

We are subjective, biased, inclined with certain leanings about it.

We are subject to it, both apprehending it and captured by it.
We are embedded in it.

At this point in the learning we are embedduals: caught in the web of our own meaning.

Then We Reflect

Almost immediately we begin the process of filtering the experience. We filter it from behind our own eyes, through who and what we are, what our past has brought us to in this particular moment. We internalize newness through our subjective feeling filter. We experience newness in the schemata of our personal world.

As we begin this filtering process, we emerge from our embeddedness in the newness and separate from it. We release our subjectivity in our need to become objective.

Then We Conceptualize

We stand back, examine, narrow our focus. We name it, conceptualize it, attempt to understand it.

We move to comprehension.

We move to objectivity,
to abstract conceptualization,
to the cognitive.

We move from percept to concept.

This separation is necessary in order to really see the newness.

Our inner feeling appraises where we are with this new thing, then our cognitive examines. We are interested, curious, intrigued.

We separate ourselves from it.
We symbolize it by naming it.
We look at what others say about it, our peers, the experts; what others have done with it; where it fits into the scheme of the larger world.

We move to comprehend it,
to have it, not to be had by it.

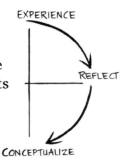

Then We Act

But comprehension is not enough.
We must try it, tinker with it, play with it, watch it, and make it work. We must do it. Now that it has become the object, we become the object manipulator.

We interact with it, we use it, we see how it works for us. First the way others do it, then in our own way.

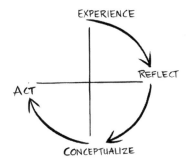

Finally We Integrate

We change it to suit us, we enrich it.

We place it in our world,
we transfer it to where we live.
We adapt it, making something new of it.

We integrate it.
We are enriched by it.

And we are transformed.

Then, and only then,
learning has happened.

Learning doesn't happen until 11:59!

This making of meaning,
which is learning itself,
is in and out,
into the self and out to the world,
over and over again.
We need to relate anew continuously
to make meaning.

"This adaptive conversation is the very source of, and the unifying content for, thought and feeling…this process is about the development of knowing."[3]

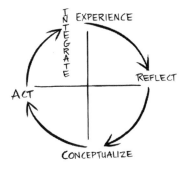

---

[3]Kegan, Robert, 1982

Piaget's Stages and the Natural Cycle

Why haven't we used this natural cycle throughout our educational history? It is not new; it has firm foundations in Jung,[4] Dewey,[5] Lewin,[6] Kolb,[7] Vygotsky,[8] and the neuroscientists.

Why do most schools still persist in the notion that only some youngsters can learn the "tough stuff," relegating the others to lower levels, so-called "basic" courses?

This is what Marc Tucker, President of the National Center on Education and the Economy, calls the "tragedy of low expectations."[9]

"The single most important obstacle to high student achievement in the United States is our low expectations for students."

How did it happen that we ignored the cycle, and decided that only some of our children could reach high skills and intellectual expertise levels?

America's psychologists announced that achievement in schools was the result of innate intelligence, and intelligence was a function of genetic endowment. Biodeterminism is an insidious notion about which Stephen Jay Gould, Professor of Biology and the History of Science at Harvard University, cautions us "to never forget the human meaning of lives diminished by these false arguments...few tragedies can be more extensive than the stunting of life, few injustices deeper than the denial of an opportunity to strive or even to hope, by a limit imposed from without, but falsely identified as lying within."[10]

And so educators came to regard those who could reach what Piaget called "formal reasoning" as the gifted ones.

Educators adopted Piaget's definitions of stages of intellectual growth as the only descriptions of growth. Logic became the gauge to measure this growth, and the linear language describing this growth became the description of the epitome of educational goals.

---

[4]Jung, Carl, 1923

[5]Dewey, John, 1938

[6]Lewin, Kurt, 1951

[7]Kolb, David, 1983

[8]Vygotsky, L. S., 1978

[9]Tucker, Marc and Judy Codding, 1998

[10]Gould, Stephen Jay, 1981

We now know that Piaget's formal reasoning is only one aspect of intelligence. The "roundness" of the right mode, discussed in Chapters Three and Four in this book, is equally important. And the processing of learning into active behavior with hands-on and adapting mechanisms must take an equal place in the current definition of intelligence. Hands-on learning can no longer be regarded as lesser talent.

Yet the schooling definition of thinking remains quite narrow. It is limited to the 6 o'clock things, the reasoning and analysis things.

And somehow that need, to teach the 6 o'clock kind of thinking, has become the **only** kind of thinking to teach.

We ask our students to stay often in the receiving mode, studying facts and analyzing, examining what the experts have done. While this is a part of all learning, it is just not enough.

With "formal thinking" as the highest level, the best thinkers are the abstract thinkers, and direct experience takes a "back seat."

Using these stages, we view children through the narrow bias of logical ability, neglecting to take into account the whole range of knowing that human experience is.

We start with the concrete and we move to the abstract. But it is not just the ability to be abstract that we are after.

Learning is active doing. Learning is problem solving, creating hypotheses, tinkering with them, drawing conclusions, and much more.

In Piaget's conception, we have a vivid description of the functions of the left cerebral hemisphere. The whole brain needs to be engaged.

There is no hierarchy on the cycle. All parts of the cycle are equally necessary and equally "intelligent." Together they comprise the wholeness of how we learn. It is not better or smarter to be at 6 o'clock. It is simply a part of the cycle. We need to return to direct experience by using what we learn.

The cycle represents how each of us learns at whatever developmental stage. The cycle describes how we move from direct experience to expert knowledge, through reflection to action, and then to integration.

Teachers must understand that all learners travel the cycle regardless of their age: they experience, reflect, conceptualize, act, and return to new experience.

The problem is that schools have overemphasized the growth and development that happens at 6 o'clock. And they have done this at the expense of the 12 o'clock ways of being and understanding.

The 12 o'clock place is a crucial, powerful place necessary for all learning. It must be included in all instructional designs.

It is where the real felt gusto of knowing happens— it is where we are embedded in the moment, with feeling and emotional engagement, a gestalt place, and unique to each individual. It is Direct Experience, where the Self begins and where the Self integrates.

It shares an equal place with abstracting.
It is the material we abstract from.

In the business world, managers are being urged to manage with heart as well as head. Team excellence depends on emotionally healthy people. A talent for rapport is the essential emotional skill for preserving close relationships. How people feel as they battle illness has a direct effect on their return to health. "We send emotional signals at every encounter."[11]

These skills grow out of expertise throughout the entire cycle.

How are our children to learn these skills, so essential for all meaningful human living, if we do not encourage them to move into their subjective insights, if we do not enlist their empathy and caring, if we do not require that they reflect on their actions and act on their reflections, if we do not engage their emotional intelligence?

To not include the 12 o'clock place in our teaching borders on malpractice.

---

[11]Goleman, Daniel, 1995

The Importance of the Entire Cycle

The 4MAT cycle is more important than any one segment.

We are in it, we are the context, we are at the center.

Each new learning, each skill, each tinkering act, processes the learning to some kind of mastery, making the understanding usable. When we use what we learn, when we perform it, it becomes integrated into our real lives, our out-of-school lives.

We begin with context, examine text, and return to context.

Our brain is a complex, adaptive, flexible, self-organizing system, shaping and reshaping itself in the interplay between ourselves and the world of experience.

And so this meaning-making is a multifaceted achievement.

Because we are also.

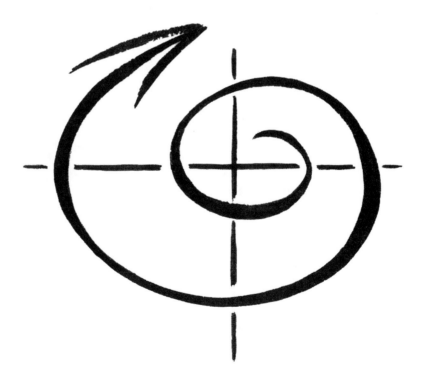

And What of the Learner?

What happens to the learners in schools if most learning activity takes place at 6 o'clock, if learners primarily sit and listen to lectures?

How does the child who needs to linger in experience fare in such schools?

And what of the child who needs more reflecting time?

How does the child fare who needs to do it to learn it?

And what of the child who doesn't take anyone's word for it, but has to find out personally?

How do all these children succeed? How are they judged?

These are legitimate learners. They are intelligent, they have a right to be who they are. They are just different.

In life outside of school, or in the world, these differences are good. They form the foundations of great and creative teams.

Schools must include them all.

Insights About the 4MAT Cycle

☆ The cycle is three-dimensional. It is really a spiral.

☆ The cycle has depth as well as height.

☆ The cycle begins and ends with the individual.

☆ The cycle is a movement from subject to object to integration, which is a powerful definition of learning.

☆ Any successfully completed cycle will flow to reflection on itself.

☆ The cycle is a consummate design for curriculum.

☆ The cycle encompasses important assessment benchmarks.

☆ The cycle is a showplace for different styles at different places.

☆ The cycle is a stretch for all who travel it.

☆ The cycle is a profound look at human growth.

However you may search for it.

You will never be able to grasp it.

You can only become it.

—Ikkyu

The Cycle is Three Dimensional:
It is Really a Spiral

Every trip around the cycle leads to more learning.

The first quadrant is making meaning,
the second quadrant is forming concepts,
the third quadrant is taking action,
and the fourth quadrant is adapting new behaviors.

Learners grow to better questions,
more complex understandings, and
develop keener eyes for new experiences.

Imagine the cycle spatially. Look at it from the side to see the spiral.
Each turn of the wheel, connecting, conceptualizing, taking action,
and integrating, brings the learner to a higher level.

From being in experience, to understanding experience,
to integrating that experience into new learning—
all forming a spiral of growth at each turn of the wheel.

Not only do we travel the cycle in continuous communication with
the external world, but we parallel that movement in concert with
our inner lives.

We make connections at two levels:
the values connection that leads to cognitive understanding
and the emotional connection that accompanies all real meaning.
The awareness time we spend with our feelings,
the courage we have to look them right in the eye,
determines the depth of meaning we attach to our learning.
This emotional learning accompanies our cognitive learning,
in an in and out rhythm around the cycle.

The Cycle Spirals Both Up and Down:
It Has Depth As Well As Height

Imagine again looking at the cycle from the side. Picture the spiral rising to new levels with each spin around. Now also imagine a cone-like shape extending down from the center.

The different activities that take place around the wheel are all facets of a key concept. The experience you create to connect meaning to your students, the presentation of the chosen content, the skills the students must practice, and the unique application made from the learning all need to be connected to this center.

Teach to the core of the learning, the essence, the structural heart of the material.

Learning is experiencing, connecting, reflecting, naming, acting, evaluating, and integrating. Never forget it is all of those things. And your conceptual choices, if they are excellent ones, connect all of this to all of your students.

But you have to know the key concepts in your content. Master teachers find and teach to these key concepts, these centers. Successful learners work at the center.

Connect the essence of your content to your students, and stand back and watch your classroom come alive.

It is the connections that give us energy.
It is the connections that give us meaning.

—David Bohm

The Cycle Begins and Ends with the Individual

All learning begins with the Self. The cycle moves from personal connections at 12 o'clock, to the knowledge of the experts at 6 o'clock, and back to the Self as the learning is personally adapted. This process transforms the learner through new understanding and skills.

The cycle is a movement from subject to object to integration, which is a powerful definition of learning.

Moving around the cycle takes us from being subjective
(embedded in the experience)
to standing outside the experience and examining it as an object
(becoming objective).

If we stay in tune with this movement of meaning,
the conversation that unifies feeling and thought continues.
We connect, we separate, and we connect anew.
We try what we have understood by acting on our conclusions,
then moving back to deeper integration each time.

This returns us to experience again.
The conversation goes on. Feeling and thought interact, and merge
the possibilities for newness and continuous learning without limit.
Learners move from subjectivity, to objectivity, to integration,
the complete learning act.

The oneness of the overall system is paramount.

—David Bohm

Any Successfully Completed Cycle will Flow to Reflection on Itself

If a cycle is completed with meaning and attention, students will naturally reflect on the entire experience. This reflection on past cycles follows whenever deep and important learning happens. Teachers need to build in reflection time and reflective activities for their learners, both during and after the cycle.

The Cycle is a Consummate Design for Curriculum

Successive cycles extend not only to the next lesson or unit, but also all the way through the curriculum. I know of no better way to structure curriculum. The cycle is useful not only for individual units, but also for designing frameworks for entire programs: kindergarten through grade 12, college, adults, corporate training. The 4MAT cycle insures conceptually coherent and balanced instruction and appeals to the legitimate diversity of all learners.

The Cycle Encompasses Important Assessment Benchmarks

The cycle frames assessment in a manageable way. Assessment is not just facts recall. But mastering the techniques that might bring comprehensive assessment programs to our learners are not well understood, let alone practiced to any degree in our schools. We need to assess meaning connections, along with verbal and nonverbal representations of concepts. We need to measure how knowledge is connected and understood relationally. We need the kinds of strategies that measure our ultimate purpose in teaching and training which is performance. Both curriculum and assessment issues will be discussed in length in Chapter Six.

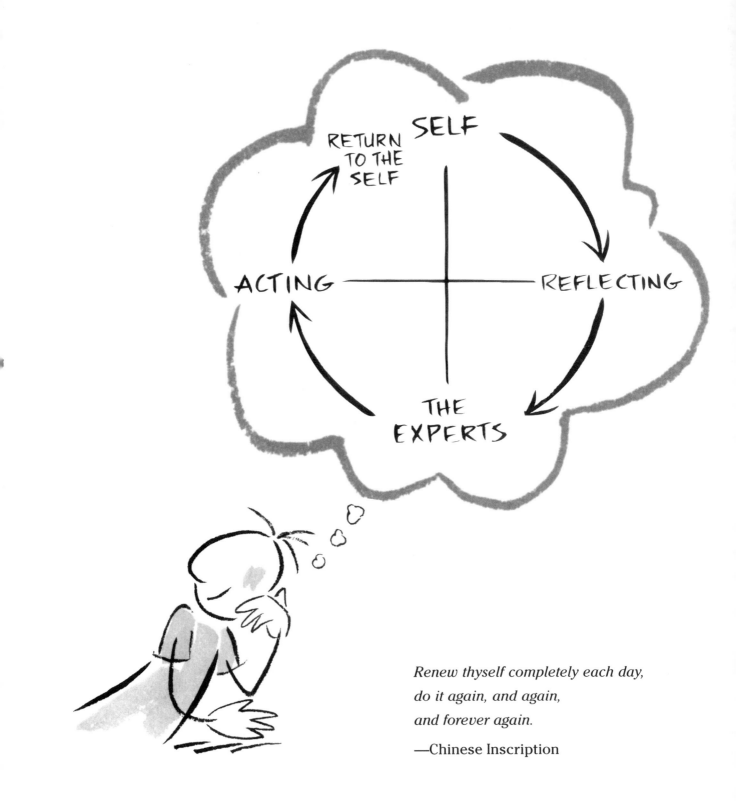

Renew thyself completely each day,
do it again, and again,
and forever again.

—Chinese Inscription

Chapter One: The 4MAT Cycle

The cycle is a showplace for different styles at different places.

Each of us shines at different places on the cycle based on our preferences. There are places on the cycle that are simply more comfortable for us than others. When we are in our comfortable place, we are graceful and sure of ourselves, we feel at home. And these places are very different for different learners.

That is why teams composed of diverse learners who trust each other are so successful, their different gifts combine to form a rich and successful complexity.

The cycle is a stretch for all who travel it.

This is true because we are comfortable in some places but challenged in others. Mastering the entire cycle is a stretch, but well worth the effort.

The cycle is a formula for human growth.

We are here to make meaning, and this cycle frames that process.

Think About Yourself

Work Task: Where are you on the learning cycle?

In an average day of 16 hours (8 hours for sleeping):

> How much time do you spend experiencing the now, what is actually happening in the moment?
>
> How much time do you spend reflecting on what has happened?
>
> How much time do you spend thinking, examining, focusing on some aspect of what interests you intellectually?
>
> How much time do you spend acting, doing the things your day demands of you?

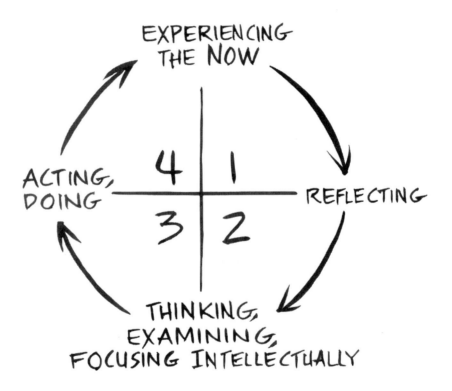

Which parts of the cycle are your strengths?

We meet ourselves
time and again
in a thousand disguises
on the paths of life.

—Carl Jung

Which needs the most improvement?

Think about the word "learning" (actively valuing and attending to some newness in your life with curiosity and excitement). How much of your day is spent in "learning"?

What one thing could you do that would improve your ability to stay in a learning mode more often?

To Do For Your Students

Bring a real experience into your classroom to introduce a new unit.

Add guided reflection to your teaching activities.

Chapter Two

The Foundation of the Cycle

When I approach a child

he inspires me in two sentiments:

tenderness for what he is,

and respect for what he may become.

—Louis Pasteur

The Foundation of the Cycle

The cycle describes the learning act itself.

We choose our most comfortable places along the two continua of perceiving and processing, and we approach learning using that favored combination.

The result of those choices determines our learning style.

If teachers understand the cycle, they can use it to powerful advantage.

Four major learning styles result from our choices along the two continua of perceiving and processing. I call them Types One, Two, Three, and Four.

There is no hierarchy. All four styles are equally excellent and legitimate.

These four styles are the result of a composite of research from learning theorists and brain research.[1]

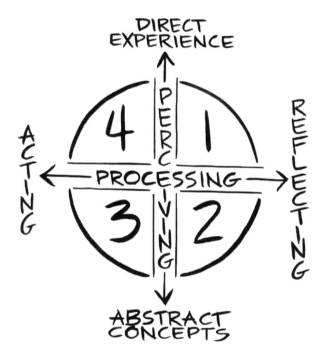

[1]Bradshaw-1983, Bogen-1986, Dewey-1938, Gardner-1985, Jung-1923, Kolb-1983, LeDoux-1996, Restak-1991, Shlain-1998, Siegel-1999, Vygotsky-1978

HONORING

Life is becoming what we are.
When a student does not learn,
the fault, in some way, belongs to the system.

—Louis Machado

Learning Styles

Particular approaches individuals have
to perceiving and processing information and experience
that result in certain preferred places on the learning cycle,
to the partial exclusion of others.

While relatively stable over time,
our style preferences are highly affected
by the situations we find ourselves in.
We do what we have to do.
But some of those situations are a real stretch.

It is critical that we learn to be flexible at those places on the cycle that are a challenge for us, even as we maintain our individual learning preferences, the special spins we put on our growth and development.

Teachers must design instruction with a framework that encompasses the cycle and honors individual differences throughout the complete learning process.

What follows in this chapter is a reiteration of learning style theory, the rationale underlying the choices learners make along the continua of perceiving and processing.

EXPERIENCE

HOW WE PERCEIVE

ABSTRACTING

How Perceiving Defines Us As Learners

We perceive things differently.
We take things in differently.
In new learning situations, some of us sense and feel our way,
staying with our direct experiences.

Others think things through,
preferring to move quickly to abstractions.

Those who perceive in a feeling way,
an intuitive way, sense the experience,
connecting the information to meaning.
They learn through the lens of the affect, the emotional.

These sensor-feelers
believe in their intuition,
They are, by their very nature, holistic.
The gestalt of Direct Experience at 12 o'clock is home to them.

On the other hand,
those who think through their experiences
tend more to the abstract.
They analyze what is happening, examining the parts.
Their intellect makes the first appraisal.
They reason experience.

Analysis necessitates
a standing outside,
an attempt to override
(although never entirely possible)
the personality of the perceiver.
This is the 6 o'clock place
where learners strive to be as free from bias as possible.

"Who could ever tire of this heart-stopping transition,
of this breakthrough shift between seeing and knowing you see,
between being and knowing you be?
It drives you to a life of concentration, it does,
a life in which effort draws you down so very deep
that when you surface you twist up exhilarated with
a yelp and a gasp."[2]

---

[2]Dillard, Annie, 1974

The particular perceiving orientation you come to favor over time,
feeling (depending largely on direct experience) or thinking
(depending largely on abstraction), is one of two major factors
determining who you are as a learner.

Both kinds of perception are equally valuable,
both have their own strengths and weaknesses.
Schools do not value the feeling approach, it is grossly neglected
(and that is even an understatement). Progression through the
grades leads learners away from feeling, dealing more and more
with abstractions about experience—botany without flowers,
astronomy without stars, life skills without emotion.

This is very frustrating for those who are feelers,
and a great loss for those who are thinkers as well.

I do in fact doubt that schooling,
as presently conceived and conducted,
is capable of providing large segments of young people
with the education they and democracy require,
and I include among these young people
a significant proportion of those now "Making it."

—John Goodlad

How Processing Defines Us as Learners

The second major difference in how we learn is how we process what we experience, what we *do* with what happens to us.

Some of us jump right in and try things, others watch what happens and reflect on it before jumping in.

Some of us reflect, some of us act.
Both approaches have their strengths and weaknesses.

Schools ask learners to watch and listen and reflect. This is frustrating for those who need to act, to do, to try things.
(This is a great loss for those who prefer to reflect as well.)

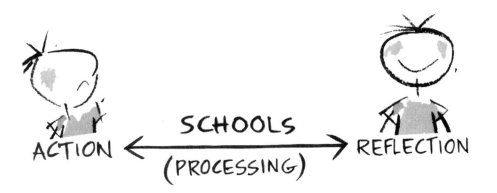

Those who prefer to reflect, filter new learnings through their own experiences. That is how they make meaning connections.

Those who prefer to act need to try things out, they need *to do it*, to extend it into their world. That is how they make meaning connections.

Even if the theory that now exists were perfect,
most of us in education have never before worked
from theory to practice...
We cannot expect the theory itself to solve our problems.
The understanding has to be applied.

Deciding what is to be abandoned is crucial...
and letting go is often much harder than taking hold.

—Leslie Hart

The Processing Dimension and John Dewey

John Dewey maintained that if learning is real, it will create purpose and direction. And that direction will lead to change, and then to transformation.

Dewey talked of the transaction between the learner and the environment. His theory of education is a theory of doing.

Dewey addressed the importance of human experience as the gateway to understanding.

Cognitive potential evolves through use.

Learning happens as we unite our experiences and their meaning with actions that test those meanings in the world.

Dewey believed we should unite mind and body through a method of thinking and doing he called "the art of education."

Schools have overlooked the wisdom of Dewey.

Think of how different our assessment strategies would be if we applied Dewey.

For example, students would have performance requirements. They would have to **do** what they learn. It would not be enough to recite information. Learners would have to make what they learn useful. They would have to show how they use it in their lives.

All children have intelligence.
We have asked the wrong question.
We ask, "How much?"
We must ask, "What kind?"

—Mary Meeker

Perceiving and Processing and Style

Our favorite places on the 4MAT cycle result in individual learner differences.

The perceiving continuum of 4MAT moves from experiencing directly (DE) to abstract conceptualizing (AC). Those of us who feel more graceful in direct experience tend to linger at 12 o'clock. Those of us who feel more graceful in conceptual abstraction tend to linger at 6 o'clock.

The processing continuum of 4MAT moves from reflection (R) to action (A). Those of us who feel more graceful in reflection tend to linger at 3 o'clock. Those of feel more graceful in action tend to rush toward 9 o'clock.

The combination of these two choices forms our individual differences. I call them:

Type One Learners,

Type Two Learners,

Type Three Learners, and

Type Four Learners.

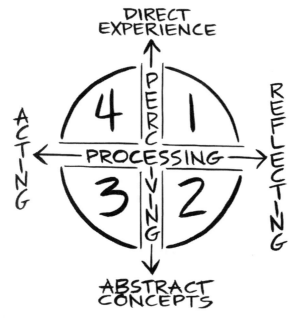

Designers of instruction at all levels, in all fields, in all settings both formal and informal, need to understand the legitimacy of these differences and design instruction to accommodate them.

Type One Learners

Perceive information directly at 12 o'clock and process it reflectively at 3 o'clock.

They learn by feeling their experiences, being present to them, trusting in their perceptions, and being open to sensory input. They take time to reflect and ponder their experience. They seek meaning and clarity. They integrate experience with the Self. They learn primarily in dialogue, by listening and sharing ideas. They excel in viewing these ideas from many perspectives. They have highly developed imaginations. They are insightful, absorbing reality, taking in the climate. They thrive on lots of reflecting time, especially when pondering new ideas. They seek commitment. They work for harmony and clue in to the needs of others with ease. They are great mentors. They nurture others to help them accomplish their goals. They tackle problems by reflecting alone and then brainstorming with others. They exercise authority through group participation. If they are forced into a conflict situation (which is usually difficult for them), they deal with it through dialogue and a great deal of listening. They build trust through personal interactions.

Their favorite question is **"Why?"**
They seek to know the underlying values.

As **Teachers** they:

- are interested in facilitating individual growth and self-awareness,
- encourage their students to be authentic,
- believe curricula should help students know themselves and others,
- see knowledge as the basis for achieving potential,
- involve their students in discussions and group projects,
- believe reflection is a primary method for enhancing self-awareness, and
- are informed about social issues that affect human development.

Strength: People skills, reflection

Goals: To be involved in important issues and to bring harmony

Need to Improve: Working under pressure and taking risks

Type Two Learners

Perceive information abstractly at 6 o'clock and process it reflectively at 3 o'clock.

They learn by thinking through experiences, judging the accuracy of what they encounter, examining details and specifics. They take the time to reflect and ponder on what they experience. They seek to achieve goals and to be personally effective. They integrate their observations into what they already know, forming theories and concepts. They excel in traditional learning environments and are thorough and industrious. They judge new learning by how theoretically sound it is. They are intrigued by how systems function. They look for structure. They thrive on stimulating lectures and readings. They seek continuity and certainty and are wary of subjective judgments. They have clearly defined goals and monitor cutting-edge research in their fields. They want to be as knowledgeable and accurate as possible. They are systematic. They tackle problems with logic and analysis. They exercise authority with principles and procedures. If they are forced into a conflict situation, they deal with it systematically, dissecting the problem before coming to a conclusion. They build trust by knowing the facts and presenting them systematically.

Their favorite question is **"What?"**
They seek to know what the experts know.

As **Teachers** they:

- are interested in transmitting the best knowledge,
- try to help their students become good thinkers,
- encourage excellence,
- believe curricula should encompass significant information with facts in service to that goal,
- see knowledge as the basis for achieving goals,
- involve their students in lectures, note taking, and readings,
- believe people should approach learning systematically, and
- are up-to-date on the expert knowledge in their content areas.

Strength: Concepts and theory, reflection
Goals: Intellectual recognition
Need to Improve: Creativity

Type Three Learners

Perceive information abstractly at 6 o'clock and process it actively at 9 o'clock.

They learn by thinking through their experiences, judging the usefulness of what they encounter. They take the time to figure out what can be done with what they learn. They seek utility and results. They integrate new learning by testing theories. They excel at down-to-earth problem solving, often tinkering to make things work. They learn best with hands-on techniques. And once they have it, they move quickly to mastery. They are pragmatists, they need closure, they like to get things done. They thrive in the company of competent people and excel at problem solving. They seek to get to the heart of things. They work for deadlines and "keep to the plan." They like to be considered competent. They help others to be competent. They tackle problems quickly, often without consulting others. They exercise authority with reward and punishment. If they are forced into a conflict situation, they deal with it by creating solutions. They build trust with straightforward forcefulness.

Their favorite question is **"How does this work?"**
They seek to know the usability of theory.

As **Teachers** they:

- are interested in helping their students achieve high skills competence,
- try to lead their students to mastery for life skills,
- encourage the practical aspects of learning,
- believe curricula should stress economic usefulness and opportunity,
- see knowledge as enabling learners to make their way in the world,
- involve their students in problem solving, experiments, and hands-on activities,
- believe their students should approach problems scientifically, and
- excel in the technical aspects of their fields.

Strength: Action, getting things done
Goals: Productivity, competence
Need to Improve: People skills

Type Four Learners

Perceive information directly at 12 o'clock and process it actively at 9 o'clock.

They learn from their perceptions and the results of their experiences. They are open to all manner of sensory input. They take the time to consider the possibilities of what they learn. They seek challenge and are risk takers. They integrate their present experiences with future opportunities. They learn primarily through self-discovery. They excel at synthesizing. They are flexible and flourish in challenging situations. They are enthusiastic about enriching reality, putting new "spins" on things. They thrive on chaotic situations. They seek to influence others. They push their potential. They are at ease with all types of people. They actively seek growth and pressure others to do so. They tackle problems with their intuition. They exercise authority by influence and expect their people to be accountable. If they are forced into a conflict situation, they react emotionally and then move to cool rationality. They build trust with high communication skills and openness.

Their favorite question is **"What If?"**
They seek to know the possibilities.

As **Teachers** they:

- are interested in enabling learners to seek possibilities,
- help their students act on their dreams,
- believe self-awareness comes from challenging oneself,
- encourage real-experience learning,
- believe curricula should be geared to individual learner interests,
- see knowledge as important to bringing about change,
- involve their students in many out-of-school activities, and
- use the community as their classroom, seeing community needs as learning opportunities.

Strength: Innovation and action for change
Goals: To be on the cutting edge of social progress
Need to Improve: Digging into the details

Work Task

What learning style do you favor?

Take the *Learning Type Measure** and follow the directions for scoring. Share your results with a friend. Discuss your style with someone whose style is different from yours.

Write your reflections here. Are you surprised? Do you agree with the findings? Did your schooling teach to your favorite style?

_____

_____

_____

_____

_____

_____

_____

_____

Using the descriptions of the four learning styles from the preceding pages, create four logos, one for each quadrant, that visually represent the essence of each of the four styles.

*If you do not have a copy, you can order one from www.aboutlearning.com or call, fax, or write About Learning, Inc., 1251 Old Rand Road, Wauconda, IL 60084. Phone 800-822-4MAT, Fax 847-487-1811.

Chapter Three

The Brain-Mind Learning System

Somewhere in the lost history of our race
we began the habit of abandoning
the integrity of our senses.
The newfound suspicion of the senses
gave us the basis for a growing infatuation with the products of conception.

Conception birthed the formal structure of thought
that finally cut us off from primary experience.
It expelled us to the wastelands of the world outside of experience.

—Bob Samples

The Brain-Mind Learning System

Introduction

The effects of genetic and environmental factors are inextricably mingled from the earliest stages of development. The remarkable combination of gene-controlled factors, some of them conserved for over a billion years, together with an enormous range of idiosyncratic factors, both internal and external, help account for the uniqueness of each individual.

—*Opening remarks at the 4th Symposium on the Human Brain*
  Arnold B. Scheibel, M.D., University of California, Berkeley, March, 1998

There is one key question to answer when we combine the findings on style with the brain research:

> *Can we design an instructional system that capitalizes on all the phases of the learning act, honoring the diversity of our students and using the best and most brain compatible techniques?*

To explore this question, we need to look further at the complexity of human beings.

We need to understand something about the uniqueness each person brings to the learning act in light of the current brain research. An examination of this research can further enhance teacher understanding as to how to accommodate style in designing instruction using teaching strategies that appeal to both left- and right-mode processing. This section deals with brain function throughout the learning act, from emotion and its impact on memory, to reasoning, to tinkering, to adapting and creating.

Emotion is a crucial aspect of humanness. It drives our everyday lives and most certainly relates to learning. The research is clear, emotional engagement needs to be part of how we teach.

Memory is connected to emotion and teachers can help their students remember important content by capitalizing on this connection.

Good teaching techniques call forth *intuitive insights,* a crucial part of the human thinking process.

Imagination and the use of mental visualizing and the creation of metaphors help our students to understand their own subjectivity as they examine expert knowledge.

The *spatial manipulation* of thought is a high form of cognitive processing with a strong engagement of the right mode. Teachers can help their students do this kind of thinking with more expertise and fluidity if they understand what it is.

Our use of *language,* the way we form our thoughts into words and the particular language we speak, limits our thinking and conceptualizing ability. Teachers need first to understand this about themselves and then bring that understanding to their students.

And finally, the culminating part of this chapter incorporates the *doing* things, the hands-on, trial and error, tinkering part of learning, the key piece of synthesizing that brings our students to adapt what they learn for their own fit, where they make what they learn work in their lives.

This litany of teaching techniques, this repertoire of strategies, is the hallmark of the master teacher. This chapter is designed to explain and illustrate these brain-compatible techniques in order to enlarge teaching repertoires to better serve all the children.

Left- and Right-Mode Processing

"The anatomic and functional separation between the two hemispheres permits their processes to be quite independent at times, and it directly shapes the construction of subjective experience."[1]

Much I reflect on the good and the true
In the faiths beneath the sun
But most upon Allah Who gave me
Two
Sides to my head, not one.
I would go without shirt or shoe,
Friend, tobacco or bread,
Sooner than lose for a minute the
Two
Separate sides of my head!

—Rudyard Kipling, 1927

This idea is not new. Our brains are double, the two sides sometimes working separately, sometimes together, each leading and following and sometimes in conflict, depending on the situation, the task, and the context.

The left- and right-mode dimensions are:

doing and being,

cognition and intuition,

objectivity and subjectivity,

analysis and synthesis,

symbolism and patterning,

sequence and simultaneity,

linear and round,

language and space.

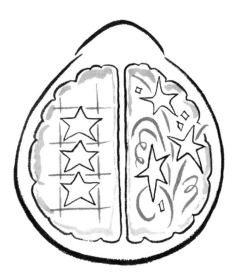

[1]Siegel, Daniel, 1999

Our greatest scientists are generally skilled in nonverbal thinking,
yet we usually discourage science students from studying artistic subjects.

Unless we reverse this trend,
they will continue to be cut off from thought processes
that lead to creative breakthroughs.

—Robert Root-Bernstein, Salk Institute

Neuroscience has illuminated the duality. Education has attempted to apply it. But the right mode remains elusive. It is not easy to describe in words. It is difficult to communicate the understanding of the right mode, simply because of the ineffable qualities of insight and intuition. The receptivity of the senses, the suspension of analysis, the quest for meaning are difficult to illuminate in precise language.

"The greater the fluency in nonverbal thought, the greater the dysfluency in verbal communication."[2]

Individuals differ regarding these two methods of approaching learning.

Robert Frost, the American poet, puts it this way:

> *"Scholars get their knowledge with conscientious thoroughness along projected lines of logic; poets theirs cavalierly and as it happens... snatching a thing from some previous order with not so much as a ligature clinging to it of the old place where it was organic."[3]*

[2]West, Thomas, 1991
[3]Frost, Robert, 1951

Many of the greatest scientists build models in their mind.

But there is also the athlete who can carry the whole game in his head—

the racing car driver who can visualize an entire race.

Such intuitive models have played a major role in the history of human survival,

and an important part of this intelligence is the ability to build accurate models of reality in one's mind.

—Thomas West

The right mode see things with the mind's eye, visualizing how the parts make up the whole, excelling in spatial skills.

The right mode sees concepts in pictures and uses these images to create metaphors that form new combinations of ideas, enabling insight leaps to sudden new knowings.

The right mode relates disparate parts, it is the great synthesizer.

To combine the best of right- and left-mode thinking is to bring learners to excellence:

the complexity of percept and concept,
understandings of both heart and head,
analysis and synthesis,
being and knowing integrated.

Take a consummate musical performance and imagine the result when the performer plays with the highest technical expertise while pouring his or her soul into the music, which is in turn resonating in the souls of the audience.

Or recall chaos theory where the shape informs the system, where the right-mode's ability to see spatially combines with the left mode's ability to master system thinking:

"Linking topology and dynamical systems is the possibility of using a shape to help visualize the whole range of behaviors of a system. Bending the shape a little corresponds to changing the system parameters...Shapes that look roughly the same give roughly the same kinds of behavior. If you can visualize the shape, you can understand the system."[4]

The right mode is not minor, not lightweight. It is high-powered understanding, and manipulating ideas spatially is one of its key characteristics. Also note the importance of the left mode in a task like the one described above. Detailed expertise maximizes the power of the corresponding visual representations. The ability to use both right and left modes skillfully needs to be a major goal of all instruction.

---

[4]Gleick, James, 1987

Frank Benson, an important writer on creativity, characterizes the ability to form concepts as:

> *"...bihemispheric, the right mode forming the visual image, the left, the semantic relationship. The combination produces a total concept."* [5]

The brain is a dynamic structure that employs both modes in a marvelously complex interplay, and its highest action is to unite the processing of the two modes.

The Brain Research

What follows is a description of right- and left-mode brain research and some teaching applications. These applications cover a much broader spectrum of learning processes than is customary in our schools, and they offer real possibilities for enhancing the potential of our students.

Hemisphericity: the concept that an individual is held to rely more on one mode of processing than another. Each of us has a favored right- or left-mode approach to processing learning.

People who approach learning with a left-mode preference are systematic. They solve problems first by looking at the parts. They are analytic planners, logical and sequential.

People who approach learning with a right-mode preference see patterns. They solve problems first by looking at the whole. They are intuitive connectors, synthesizers.

The goal of education is to develop the flexible use of both of these processing modes, instructing and encouraging students to use their whole brain systems by allowing time for:

- lecturing and interacting,
- picturing and naming,
- demonstrating and letting them do it,
- following a sequence to check on a known reaction,
- tinkering in a self-discovery mode, and
- answering queries and creating new questions.

---

[5]Benson, Frank, 1985

Katherine Sherwood, the victim of a massive stroke, today has a career in art that is thriving as never before. Ms. Sherwood, paralyzed on her right side (left brain) has taught herself to paint left-handed (right brain). The result has been work that has made her one of the art world's rising stars.

"Her work has been radically transformed. It is rare to see work that impressive, fresh, and powerful," says Larry Rinder, curator of contemporary art at New York's Whitney Museum.

"Her left hand enjoys an ease and grace with the brush that her right hand never had—raw, intuitive, pure intent. Her paintings are breathtaking."

It is possible, neuroscientists say, that the hemorrhage remapped circuitry inside her head in a way that strengthened her more artistic right side.

–*Wall Street Journal,* May 12, 2000

We need to be aware not only that our students have different strengths when it comes to right- and left-mode processing, but also of the kinds of tasks we ask of them.

Sometimes the task calls for more right-mode involvement, sometimes more left. The key is the division of labor, what is called "task hemisphericity."[6]

There are certain tasks where the right mode excels, and others where the left mode excels.

A group of students asked to perform a left-mode task (remembering a list of names) will revert to left-mode processing. And the reverse is true. Ask for a task where the right mode excels and students will revert to their right modes.

But what happens to youngsters when we only ask them to do left-mode tasks?

---

[6]Bogen, Joseph, 1986

The brain is an intricate network of connected neurons. When the circuits of neurons fire when learning occurs, that action "alters the probability of certain patterns firing in the future. If a certain pattern has been stimulated in the past, the probability of activating a similar profile in the future is enhanced. If the pattern is fired repeatedly, the probability of future activation is further increased... the network learns from past experiences. The increased probability of firing a similar pattern is how the network remembers."[7]

How much does it affect a students' whole brain processing if they are continually asked to sequence, to name, to remember names, to relate verbally, to break down into parts, to follow procedures that lead in similar directions, and to repeat what they have been told? How much does this emphasis on left-mode processing affect the ability to synthesize, to hunch, to intuit, to tinker and play with ideas, to visualize in pictures, to polish and refine the skills of their right modes?

What is important is that we create real thinkers for our world, not just those who can rattle off information and tell us what the world already knows!

[7]Siegel, Daniel, 1999

The Left Mode

Operates with analysis, examines cause and effect.

Breaks things down into parts, examines and categorizes.

Seeks and uses language and symbols. Needs to know what things are. (The structure of the English language promotes and reinforces left-mode strategies.)

Abstracts experience for comprehension, generates theory, creates models.

Is sequential, works in time. (Time is the quintessential characteristic of the left mode.)

Some key left-mode words to remember...

Comprehension, Parts, Categories, Cause and effect, Linearity, Grids, Sequence, Reason, Words, Next

The left mode is interested in knowing those things we can describe with precision, classifying, discriminating, and naming.

It is...

- A great technical text
- When the statistics confirm
- The best verbal directions
- Hearing exactly what was said
- Edges
- Time
- Reason
- Nouns
- Processing through analysis to construct detailed representations
- Text (as opposed to context)
- It has a drive to explain.

The Right Mode

Operates out of being, intuits feeling states.

Understands and honors wordlessness.

Sees wholes, forms images, mental combinations.

Seeks and uses patterns, relationships, discrepancies, connections.

Functions visuo-spatially—
manipulating forms, distances, space.
Is simultaneous.

Some key right-mode words to remember…

Apprehension, Wholes, Images, Patterns, Relationships, Discrepancies, Simultaneity, Insights, Subjectivity, Nonverbal

It perceives the world, how it is, using a bottom-up perspective. The right mode knows more than it can tell, filling gaps, thinking aside, imaging.

It is…

- A great storyteller
- A consummate musical moment
- Elegant and simple diagrams of how something works
- Reading body language and tone of voice
- The centers, nubs
- "In the zone," street sense
- Poetry, painting with words
- Verbs
- Processing through synthesis to assess gestalt
- Context rather than text
- It sees things as they are, does not try to explain.

The essence of the left mode is linear.
The essence of the right mode is round.

Some learners who are at ease in round thinking have trouble
describing what they think.
The imagery of poetry suits them better where words become
holograms and metaphors connect and explain.
They struggle with words to express what they understand.
They know more than they can tell.

Other learners are at ease with the linear.
They describe what they mean with precision
(and are proud they can do so).
They are frustrated with ambiguity and roundness.
They seek to specify, to account for, to make distinctions.

Both kinds of learners need to enhance their gifts.
Both need to be honored for being who they are and what they
bring.

Teachers need to develop instructional methods that teach in and
to both modes.

The goal of education needs to be whole-brain flexibility,
encouraging divergent and convergent thinking, merged with the
theoretical and the intuitive, and presented with conceptual rigor.

Well-functioning adults reveal a coordinated functioning of both
hemispheres.

Right and Left: the Two Hemisphere Continuum

Left Mode	Right Mode
Is concerned with doing	Is concerned with being—one's existential state at a given moment
Specialized for speech	Specialized for visual/spatial
Analysis	Synthesis
Linear progression–time is the quintessential left-mode characteristic	Simultaneity
Attends only to the right field	Encompasses both left and right fields—attends with a broad searchlight

The following continua of right- and left-mode characteristics is relative, not absolute. Teachers, please note how few right-mode techniques are active in current teaching practice.

As you examine this list, imagine how you might bring more right-mode teaching strategies into your classroom.

Knowing

Left	Right
Is the seat of logical thought	Is the seat of feeling integration
Knows the world through symbols	Knows the world through images
Is rational	Has intuitive insights
Has a drive to explain, to create interpretations and conclusions based on selected details without relational meanings	Sees things as they are with little alteration, creates a context representation
Engages in top-down processing	Uses a bottom-up perspective
Looks at the parts	Sees the whole, the gestalt
Is field independent	Is field sensitive
Thinks first	Is more spontaneous
Uses linear time, sequence	Is simultaneous
Analyzes	Synthesizes
Controlled, systematic experiments	Open-ended, random experiments
If-then thinking, invented the idea of "next"	Networks the whole as it relates
Tends to singular focus	Tends to focus on multiples at the same time
Breaks down to the discrete	Assembles parts together
Folds new information into pre-existing world view	More attracted to paradigm shifts
Produces coherence, shuts out threatening facts	Questions the way things are
Ignores discrepancies that don't fit	Monitors discrepancies

Language

Left	Right
Sends out logical, sequential statements to interpret and make sense of things	Sends out nonverbal messages via facial expressions, gestures, and tones of voice
Negotiates an external world of symbols	Negotiates with images, body sensations, and intuitive insights that often defy words
Is into grammar and syntax	Cues in on inflections, nuances
Is verbal	Is highly nonverbal
Prefers talking and writing	Prefers drawing and manipulating
Specialized for syntax and structure	Specialized for metaphors, similes, proverbs, parables, and analogies
Efficient at processing routine codes	Efficient at processing novel situations
Cues in on the literal	Cues in on the unspoken, the emotional
Selects single meanings for words	Holds many different meanings for words
Understands the text	Understands the context

Emotion

Left	Right
Processes by appraising	Processes by connecting to arousal
Plays a major role in labeling	Plays a major role in mediating emotion, subjective awareness

(Both must be interwoven for any real understanding)

Left	Right
Words generated to another are a left-brain-to-left-brain communication	Emotional attunement to another is a right-brain-to-right-brain communication
Excels at social emotions, meets the needs of social situations	Excels at basic emotions, is aware of and responds to feelings
Avoids emotional messages	Creates an image of the other's mind, tunes in
Is relatively able to conceal emotions	Fidgets, blushes, smirks
Is serious	Is humorous
Doesn't get that upset	Gets emotionally involved
Is a conformist	Is more into disorder and change

*Learning is natural, pleasurable, spontaneous to the brain.
If that is not true, something is wrong.*

—Richard Restak

Memory: the way the brain is affected by experience

Left

Organized with vertical integration, intraregional links

Remembers facts

Can speak with ease

Remembers descriptions and parts

Remembers language, rules

Right

Organized with horizontal integration, a contextual pattern

Remembers the Self across time

Often has difficulty speaking if only the left mode of another is listening, needs another right mode

Remembers positions and distances

Remembers events

Music

Left

Strengths are duration, temporal order, sequencing, rhythm

Right

Strengths are tones, timbres, melodies

(Unprofessionally trained individuals prefer the left ear when listening to music. Professionals enjoy both the melodic qualities and analyze the music as they listen.)

"It is indisputable that there are two profoundly different modes in which the mind processes information. One or the other mode can dominate our conscious experience at various times.

"The finding that these modes of the mind do indeed have robust correlations with the sides of the brain just helps us to understand the probable neurophysiological mechanisms underlying what has been known for hundreds of years."[8]

---

[8]Benson, Frank, 1985

You've got to get all of the combinations out of your head,
so you can look at the whole structure,
to go beyond it.

Good representation is a release from intellectual bondage.

—Jerome Bruner

Any experiences that help to develop the processing abilities of both hemispheres will improve individuals' internal and interpersonal lives.

Student Learning Strategy Preferences

Those Who Favor the Left Mode	Those Who Favor the Right Mode
Prefer verbal instructions	Prefer demonstrated instructions
Like controlled, systematic experiments	Like open-ended experiments
Prefer problem solving with logic	Prefer problem solving with hunching
Find differences	Find similarities
Like structured climates	Like fluid and spontaneous climates
Prefer established information	Prefer elusive, ambiguous information
Rely heavily on the verbal	Rely on the nonverbal
Like discrete information recall	Like narratives
Control feelings	Are free with feelings
Are intrigued with theory	Need experiences
Excel in propositional language	Excel in poetic, metaphoric language
Draw on previously accumulated information	Draw on unbounded qualitative patterns, clustering around images

Uniting the activities
of the two hemispheres
is the highest
and most elaborate activity of the brain.

—Richard Restak

Work Task

From the lists on the preceding pages, choose one pair of descriptors from any category:

Knowing, Language, Emotion, Memory, or Music

Then choose a topic from one of your favorite content areas.

Next, choose a favorite grade or age level.

Then create one teaching strategy for your chosen topic that will connect your students to that content.

Choose one that would encompass both sides of the continuum you choose.

_____

_____

_____

_____

Share your strategy with a colleague.

Next, choose either a left-mode or right-mode descriptor from one end of any continuum, and create a teaching strategy that will engage only that one characteristic. There are times when your students need more practice at one end of the continuum than another. The techniques you decide to use depend entirely on your purpose, and that purpose is based on what you determine your students need.

The only caveat is that you seek balance.

_____

_____

_____

_____

Teaching Strategies that Favor the Right Mode

The following is a list of ideas for different techniques and strategies teachers can use to capitalize on the processing skills of the right mode.

Using metaphors and similes

Using metaphors may be one of the most rewarding right-mode activities, because of the possible payoff. When we create a metaphor, we must understand the core of something in order to contrast it with something else. Try answering these yourself:

> How is a tree like a poem? What metaphor will describe best for you the meaning of an algorithm?

Creating metaphors also sends you to the essence.

> What is the heart of the meaning of Huck Finn? The process of photosynthesis?

Mindmapping

These are stream of consciousness drawings where one idea presents another, and another. Ideas are drawn as they seem to relate to each other, using various shapes and directions. Both vertical operations are used, as in sets and subsets, as well as horizontal lines to indicate relationships.

A Student Sample on "My Time"

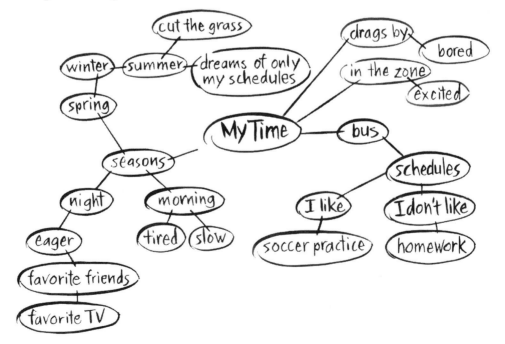

Nonverbal representations of all types

Use symbols, shapes, literal representations and nonliteral representations (squiggles, vortex type delineations, etc.) to illustrate understanding.

Example: Use a nonverbal series of just lines, no literal pictures, to capture what you think is the essence of the short story, *A Separate Piece.*

Patterning

Seeing patterns in ideas, texts, and all manner of visuals, looking at the whole to discern similarities and repetitions. Encourage your students to see the discrepancies in patterns as well.

Example: Create a record of how you spend your time, when you get home from school until you go to bed, for five school nights. Describe any pattern you see, comment on how happy you are with what you see, and suggest possible options for what you might want to change.

Using imagery

Create pictures of concepts, relationships, and connections. Put thoughts into three-dimensional space to better understand associations, links, and overall coherence. Figurative language provides intensity as well as clarification, helps to illuminate an idea, to forge comparisons.

Example: Depict the essay you wrote on justice, the police, and teenagers with images you believe explain your thinking and your feelings on the subject. You may use magazine images or your own original ones. Be sure your feelings are clear to the observer of your work.

Raising sensory awareness

Using techniques that call on auditory, visual, kinesthetic, tactile, and olfactory (smell) senses as a key to more enriched understanding and to add perspective from different angles.

Example: Find music that sounds like joy, or melancholy, or triumph. Explain what made it so. Or dance the meaning of startling change. Or tell me what anger smells like. Or create a texture that feels like competition.

Poetic language

All the uses of poetic language: metrics (the way a line breathes), pattern and sound merging, balance and design, rhyme and energy, all these can be used to create images that tell so much more than mere literal text. Poetic language can be used in many more content areas that one would think. It is a truly fine match to some areas of mathematics, for instance. It can be an excellent technique for aiding understanding, especially with students who seem to naturally gravitate to that type of language.

Example: Describe the Doppler effect with only rhyming nouns, no verbs.

Analogies

These can be drawings or words or images that represent comparisons based on similarities.

RAGE

HAPPINESS

SERENITY

HOPELESSNESS

Each of us has an outer and an inner mental life—the former uses ordinary language, but the latter cannot be expressed in words because of its complexity. So the goal is to use visual rather than verbal language to make these complex things, the human interactive things, visible, to give them form.

"Art can convey thought in such a way as to make it directly perceptible."

—Max Bill in *The Mathematical Approach to Art.*

Example: Analogies can help students capture the essence of things. For example, "Draw an analogy for the core idea of the short story you just read."

The use of paradox: a statement exhibiting inexplicable or contradictory aspects, patterning balance and tensions in both verbal and nonverbal compositions.

Ask students, "What if the exact opposite is true, what would that be like?" Find ways to have your students illustrate the balance and the lack of balance that often exist together in compositions of all kinds—an invitation to take a deeper look. Examine the profound truth concerning balance in the universe. Use the behavior of subatomic systems to illustrate.

Three-dimensional tasks

All manner of building assignments, but not limited to only concrete tasks. Ask your students to create their answers in three dimensions to the essential questions you pose in your major units. Have them build forms to illustrate their ideas and to show meanings.

Example: Create a three-dimensional version of a core belief in a certain culture. This assignment would lead your students to examine the artifacts of that culture more closely.

Dramatics, role-playing

All form of role-playing and creative dramatics. These engage the senses, visual, auditory, kinesthetic, etc. The creation of scripts involves interpersonal understandings. Have them build storylines that illustrate building tensions among individuals, and so on. This technique has so many positives, including great fun. Why teachers do not use it more is a real puzzle to me.

Example: Create a role-play wherein one of you is the father, and one the son who just received a very poor report card. And it is the first half of the son's senior year. (I actually did this one with a class of high school seniors, and the results were not only profound, but also hilarious. Much good came out of that exchange that day.)

Clustering disparate things or ideas into new groupings or formations

This is the metaphor idea again. Putting multiple, seemingly "dis-alike" things together in new ways is a challenge to the creative mode, and a fine way to achieve new insights.

Example: How is a corporation like a garden? like a train station? like plaster?

Movement, kinesthetic strategies

Ask your student to demonstrate understandings with body motion, especially without words. This reveals the underlying meanings of ideas. I remember a group of high school seniors who "performed" the process of photosynthesis in complete silence. Ask them today all these years later what they remember about that science class and they will say, "We remember photosynthesis."

Geometry

The measurements and relationships of points, lines, angles, surfaces, and solids. The spatial dimension of geometry puts it in a class by itself, so different from the left-mode processing of algebra. Notice the students who seem to take to geometry naturally. Some will tell you it is absolutely fascinating to them. There may be two entirely different ways to approach math, the logical algebraic way and the visual-spatial way. Use the visual spatial skills of geometry to examine illustrations of relationships in other content areas. Have your students demonstrate the essence of one of their essays visually. They can use circles within circles, arrows connecting parts, etc. An interesting fact that in spite of the troubles in school experienced by Einstein, Edison, and DaVinci, they all shared a common trait, a natural interest and ability in geometry.

Most math conceptualizing

The mathematical thinker is one who above all is a student of puzzle forms. There are right- and left-mode aspects in the teaching of math. Set up discovery, bring forth the courage in your students to trust their own intuition (which precedes proof). Teach students to translate intuitive ideas into mathematical statements that can be tested.

Math presents the most exciting possibilities for whole brain strategies, and yet sadly, most math is taught in only left-mode ways. "It is the intuitive mode that yields hypotheses quickly, interesting combinations of ideas before their worth is known. The intuitive insight is exactly what the techniques of analysis and proof are designed to test and check. It is founded on a kind of combinatorial playfulness...depending in great measure on the confidence one has in the process rather than on the right answers."[9]

Consider the math of music, of poetry, of great writing.

Finding similarities across diverse domains

If the teacher conceptualizes the issues well, the big ideas will present engaging combinations that students will discover across disciplines.

Example: If the concept is "change," have students in your social studies class illustrate the concept from three different disciplines: science, human development theory, and their own community life.

Scanning is a vital skill students need to master if they are to become adults who understand "the big picture" as well as the details. "Our left brains have become stiff with technique, far from the scanning eye."[10] Teach them to skim certain texts for the main idea, to scan a complicated work of art for just a few moments and then tell each other what they saw. Have them find patterns in the way their fellow students mingle and talk and act on a minimally supervised playground.

[9]Bruner, Jerome, 1962, 1979
[10]Bruner, Jerome, ibid

Demonstrations

The act of presenting information in ways that have to be used, rather than just explained, calls upon a plethora of expertise. They need good visuals, or working models. They need to interact with their audience, and possess a real grasp of the material they are presenting. Create specific rubrics (lists of criteria) for exemplary demonstrations.

Tinkering–all kinds

Encourage your students to tinker. Give them permission to find things out for themselves. Set up experiments with many different possible and equally good results and conclusions. Their right brains will thank you.

Stream of consciousness: writing, thinking, journaling

Encourage this most subjective action as worthwhile and insightful. Let your students know that they know more than they know. Teach them to learn to trust their perceptions and emotions without worrying about whether something is said well or perfectly. The refinements come later, the insights are key here.

Using music to accompany, compare, augment, or even explain

Seldom used well, even by music teachers. Think of explaining a short story with a musical composition that illustrates the same mood, issues, or emotion. For example, "It is generally agreed that Mozart used G minor to express melancholy. The Greeks linked certain musical modes to particular emotions."[11] Have your students take a main emotion from a piece of literature and match it to a piece of music. "Musical training is a more potent instrument than any other, because rhythm and harmony find their way into the inward places of the soul, resulting in gracefulness."[12]

Use music to set tones in your classrooms. What kind of music would you use to introduce binomials in algebra, what kind to introduce James Joyce's "The Dubliners" in Senior Lit? How can you incorporate popular music (the music your students listen to) into your classroom?

---

[11]Storr, Anthony, 1992
[12]Socrates, as reported in Storr, 1992

Using color and tone to illustrate, to compare, to enrich

Use color to describe a person, a poem, a story, an idea.

Example: If you had to choose a color to describe Huck Finn, what might it be? Would Tom Sawyer be a different color?

Parallel processing

Juxtaposing ideas (side by side) to better understand both.

Example: Put the idea of chaos side by side with the idea of order. Can you find order in chaos and chaos in order? How? Give examples.

Hunching

Encourage your students to hunch. Set up situations where hunching is valued, and help them analyze the steps they follow in order to confirm or rule out their hunches. An experiment in science, or an idea about why someone acted the way they did, followed by an interview to confirm or rule out, or a search for the root cause of a complicated problem.

Body language

All manner of body language skills engage the right mode. Your students will love it! Ask them in what situations they really need to understand body language and then have them simulate such situations for each other. The result is very insightful and goes much deeper into inter- and intra-personal intelligence issues.

Reflective dialogues in which language is used to focus on the mental states of others.

What was the main character feeling during this scene? If you were in that situation, what would you be feeling? Use this technique not only to understand literature, but also to create original dramatic presentations.

Alice laughed.
"There's no use trying," she said.
"One cannot believe impossible things."
"I daresay you haven't had much practice," said the Queen.
"When I was your age, I always did it for half an hour a day. Why, sometimes I've believed in as many as six impossible things before breakfast!"

—Lewis Carroll

Autobiographical memories with emotional meaning

Have your students focus on memorable events in their lives, even perhaps those that were turning points. The understandings from these insights may be used in a variety of ways, in original stories and dramatic presentations, juxtaposed beside a hero or heroine in a literature piece, or even examined through the lens of a musical piece. Students come to insightful understandings when they return to events that had great meaning. Ask a group of students to recount such events to each other and have them create a short drama together illustrating a composite of these events.

This is a very powerful process. Your students will learn much from each other.

Polysemantic images of the world

Ask your students to create many meanings for one word. For example, words like gist, wonder, sweet, snow, fence, major. This is a fine strategy to get students to open themselves to many possible answers, to see more than single meanings from ideas and words.

Also use combinations of all those techniques listed here adding many of your own.

A Caveat

Do not confuse the lack of left-mode development with a notion that the student has a superior right mode. This may not be true. Left-mode skills are often not taught well. An inordinate amount of time is spent on facts recall and simple yes-no answers to complicated questions. The left mode requires rigor, the skills of analysis and logic, and systematic attention to the structure of content.

Comprehending significant knowledge and its accompanying meaning is a complicated duet. Excellence in both left- and right-mode teaching strategies is essential for this to happen.

How balanced is your everyday teaching practice between:

- doing and being,
- cognition and intuition,
- objectivity and subjectivity,
- analysis and synthesis,
- symbolism and patterning,
- sequence and simultaneity,
- linear and round problem solving.

Write your reflections on this question and share with a colleague.

_____

_____

_____

_____

_____

_____

Chapter Four

Further Dimensions of Brain Research:
A Deeper Look at Applications

Further Dimensions of Brain Research: A Deeper Look at Applications

The following pages offer some important brain research and ideas for classroom application in the areas of: emotion, memory, intuition, imagining and the use of metaphor, spatial intelligence, symbolism and language, tinkering and acting, and adapting and creating.

Emotion and the Brain

Emotion is the nexus for learning. It is the core of our lives. Emotion directs energy to the brain-forming connections that lead to meaning. How students feel and the meaning they elicit from what they experience determines the focus and attention they give to learning tasks. The body, the brain, and emotions are interwoven.

"An experience may be so exciting emotionally as almost to leave a scar on the cerebral tissues."[1]

Early positive emotional relationships from caring adults form the basis of learning. There is abundant evidence now that infant brains respond highly to stimulation from caregivers with changes in their organization.[2]

Emotions are feeling states that depend on meaning. Our feelings are what we are about. They are woven through all our experiences. We remember the things that are important to us. Meaning amplifies memory. Motivation directs our attention and our emotions commentate, engaging in introspective conversations. We react and evaluate. The stronger the degree of feeling, the more lasting the learning.

[1]James, William, 1899
[2]Aitken and Trevarthen, 1997

Teachers need to engage their students emotionally. They need to create feeling-laden connections for their learners, connections that intrigue and stimulate. They need to capitalize on how emotion generates new networks in the brain. These connections are made throughout all focused learning, but are especially crucial at the beginning of every major unit.

☆ Emotions motivate, address our attention, bring focus.

☆ Emotions are inherently integrative, forming functional links.

☆ Emotions signal us to discover the discrepancies that further learning will unravel.

☆ Emotion is the essence of the mind.

Emotional intelligence is self-awareness, motivation, empathy, social skills, and the positive regulation of our emotional lives.[3] As you will see in the next chapter, the first four are characteristic of the Quadrant One part of the 4MAT cycle. Quadrant One is the place on the 4MAT wheel where teachers use motivational strategies, where students engage in empathic listening and collaborative learning. When the teacher creates a climate where subjectivity is honored, and listening is attuned and personal, students make connections. The learning is powerful.

Your task as a teacher is to nurture self-awareness, to motivate, to inspire compassionate listening, to bring relevance to your content. You need to get the attention of your students at the heart level. Boredom is fatal to brain cells. Serve the brain an enriched diet and it will form new networks, new connections. You need to merge your content knowledge with the knowledge of who your students are. In order to do this, you must know them.

How many times in any classroom do students make emotional, meaning connections to the content under study? How many times in your classroom?

---

[3]Goleman, Daniel, 1995

We have learned that every part of the nerve cell
alters its dimensions in response to the environment...
Decreased stimulation will diminish a nerve cell's dendrites,
and increased stimulation will enlarge the dendritic tree...
In fact at every age studied, we have shown anatomical
effects due to enrichment or impoverishment.

—Marian Diamond[4]

[4]Diamond, Marian, 1988

Some Research Findings on Emotion and the Brain

Daniel Siegel, Clinical Professor of Psychiatry at the UCLA School of Medicine, believes the quality of interpersonal communication between a baby and his parents is of crucial importance in determining brain differentiation.

Right hemisphere development dominates early childhood. Siegel proposes that the lack of positive emotional communication may hamper this development. The primary function of the right hemisphere is mediating emotions: nonverbal communications, facial expressions, subtleties, tone of voice, and feeling attunements. If a child is deprived of this, it may well negatively affect his or her development throughout life.

What teaching strategies and techniques do the following findings suggest to you?

1. Depressed parents reduce an infant's ability to experience joy and excitement. Can we bring joy and excitement to our students?

2. Early trauma may increase the release of stress hormones in response to life experiences. Can we create stress-free classrooms?

3. The way we evaluate what happens to us is based on our experiences and the emotions that were sparked by those experiences. Can we bring the subjectivity of our students' past learning into our classrooms?

4. Emotional engagement enhances learning. Does your teaching engage your students with meaning and feeling?

5. Metacognition (awareness of our thoughts and feelings) enhances flexibility to self-regulate our emotional lives. How often do you ask your students to think about how they think and feel?

6. "Feeling felt" is a Siegel phrase for being understood, being in authentic communication (which he claims is one person's right brain in tune with another). It enhances the ability to have close, meaningful relationships throughout life. What does this finding mean for successful learning?

7. The ability to regulate one's emotions is at the core of the self. It is the result of caregivers who exhibit sensitivity to youngsters and engage in authentic communication and reflective dialogue. Do you exhibit sensitivity to your students and engage them in authentic communication and reflective dialogue?

Our sense of ourselves depends crucially
on the subjective experience of remembering our past.

—Daniel Schacter

A Note About Memory and the Brain

We remember what has meaning. We remember those things that affect not only our heads, but our hearts. Memory and emotion are inextricably bound together.

The strength of memories depends on the degree of emotional activation induced by the learning.

We remember initial perceptions that went deep, that resonated, that somehow touched something already there. We remember words that we attached to concepts that had meaning for us. We remember procedures that were immediately useful. We remember events that had emotional impact, that changed us, that altered our perceptions. These are all unique experiences that depend on our history.

It is important for teachers to create teaching applications that tap into the benefits of the way the brain remembers. Memory is a major factor in forming associations, which is where the brain excels. Attach your content to meaning and your students will remember what you teach.

Raise awareness in your students as to how they really feel, their expectations, their preconceived notions. Raise questions about their own notions and prejudices.

All strategies and techniques that lead to better questions, that illuminate complexity where the simple formerly reigned, that illustrate paradox, that lead to awareness and a deeper understanding are grist for discussion and will impact on memory if the connections are there. Begin every major teaching unit with meaning. Connect the everyday lives of your students to your content and you will insure long-term memory effects.

The most important finding from the brain research on memory is the connection to emotion. We start with ourselves and we return to ourselves. It is the way people learn, and the way the brain works.

How many different kinds of memory enhancements do you use in your teaching? How many more could you use?

As I used to say to my clients,

"Memory is life."

—Saul Bellow, the Bellarosa Connection

Work Task

List three strategies you can use to enhance your students' memory of important knowledge. Think about both left- and right-mode strategies.

1. _____

_____

2. _____

_____

3. _____

_____

Here we touch the enigmatic two-fold nature of the ego
...I am a human being cast out into the world and its individual fate;
on the other hand light which beholds itself, intuitive vision,
whose consciousness is pregnant with images that endow meaning,
and the world opens up.

—Hermann Weyl, *Mind and Nature*

Intuition

Antonio Damasio,[5] Professor of Neurology at the University of Iowa, speaks of consciousness as "feeling moments" when we form images of something new in our minds and know wordlessly it has changed us.

Nel Noddings[6] speaks of intuition as a way of knowing, a process of creating pictures in our minds to come to understanding—a process that needs to permeate the entire learning act—from perceiving to conceiving to acting to integrating.

Domasio's perspective is that of a neurologist, Noddings' that of an educator with an abiding passion for enhancing the place of intuition as an essential educational concept. They both describe how we come to know.

Intueri: to look upon, to see within, to contemplate.

The act or faculty of knowing directly, without the use of rational processes.

- Intuition is deep knowing.

- It is the voice of our insight interacting with the world.

- It is tight, intense focus.

- Immediate and direct, an unconscious source of knowledge.

- It provides the foundation for experience.

- Educators, by and large, have left it out of the teaching enterprise.

In order to motivate students to attend to learning, we must make them come alive. We need to appeal to their senses, connect to their lives, involve them in wanting to learn the material. We need to engage them, create the clearings deep within that ignite their inner knowing, set up receiving climates so they can move through the learning process with their own motivation.

---

[5]Damasio, Antonio, 1999

[6]Noddings, Nel and Paul Shore, 1984

Chapter Four: Further Dimensions of Brain Research

Truth is within ourselves, it takes no rise

From outward things, whate'er you may believe

…and to know

Rather consists in opening out a way

Whence the imprisoned splendour may escape,

Than in effecting entry for a light

Supposed to be without.

—Robert Browning

People create unique and highly subjective representations of all they encounter. The premature use of analytic thinking will hamper student freedom to hear their own past, to create their own structures.

The inner voice is the intuitive voice, and granted it is not always "on the money," but it is "seeing and wanting to see, and feeling and wanting to feel."[7]

If you want high motivation from your students, you must encourage their inner voices. Tap into the things they know without knowing they know them. The intuitive means more belief in one's own insights, more creative ideas leading to better decisions.

The goal of analysis is to prove something, to finish something. Intuition's goal is to find meaning. Teachers tend to be more at ease with finished things, not with things in process.

What are some of the means to encourage and enhance your students' intuition?

1. Modalities: engaging auditory, visual, and kinesthetic senses

2. Images of all kinds

3. Direct and immediate contact with what they are learning

"The hallmark of the intuitive experience is seeing without glasses, hearing without filters, touching with the ungloved hand."[8]

4. Metaphors, similes, and analogies

5. Inductive as well as deductive thinking

6. Strategies that require discovering hidden details

7. Stream of consciousness techniques

8. Affective dialogues concerned with feelings and insights

9. Personal narratives

10. Reflections on events from the past where intuition was strong and correct

---

[7]Noddings, Nel, 1984
[8]Noddings, Nel, ibid

It is always with excitement that I wake up in the morning
wondering what my intuition will toss up to me,
like gifts from the sea.
I work with it and rely on it. It's my partner.

—Jonas Salk

Strategies that are not conducive to intuition:

1. Highly structured settings
2. Premature movement to analysis
3. Premature evaluation of products

It is not enough to use the methods above to encourage the intuitive, without the search for meaning as the ultimate goal. The teacher's task is to set up the climate, the situation, the parameters, the concrete experiences that will move students to a quest for their own meaning.

"We cannot give meaning, it is for our students to create their own meaning. Perhaps in trying to give meaning, we actually destroy the intuitive mode, taking away the very mechanism for creating meaning in our desire to short-circuit the process for our students, an impossible task and a cruel attempt to rob them of their own experience."[9]

In our attempts to pull students quickly into the content, we rob them of the chance to call upon their own experience. We need to set up the climate where personal valuing can flourish. As the value of the learning becomes theirs, they will merge the energy of their intuition with their reasoning power. Such synergy results in deep levels of comprehension.

Noddings speaks of the creative tension between subjective certainty and objective uncertainty–when you know something in your heart and mind, yet need to examine the issues and details more closely. You are sure, yet you stay open enough to see the issues from many sides. This is the act of living in the creative tension that Nodding speaks of. She extols teachers to keep this tension active and exciting in the minds and hearts of their students.

"If the intuitive mode ends successfully, skepticism with respect to the result of incipient product vanishes and only questions concerning execution remain."[10]

----

[9]Noddings, Nel, 1984
[10]Noddings, Nel, ibid

Chapter Four: Further Dimensions of Brain Research

If we doubt its capacities or mistrust its contributions,
we make intuition, in effect, hesitant.
Its appearances will be erratic and its input ambiguous.

On the other hand, acceptance and confidence create receptivity.
If we issue an open invitation and make intuition feel that visits
are welcomed at any time, it can become a perfect guest,
showing up on all the right occasions, dressed properly and bearing
felicitous gifts.

—Philip Goldberg

Intuitive People Tend to Be...

⭐ unconventional and comfortable about being unconventional

⭐ confident

⭐ self-sufficient

⭐ emotionally involved in abstract issues, both intellectual issues and human values

⭐ able to entertain doubts and uncertainties without fear

⭐ willing to take criticism and challenge

⭐ able to accept or reject criticism, whichever the case

⭐ willing to change if they see the need

⭐ resistant to outside control

⭐ independent

⭐ foresighted

⭐ spontaneous

Encourage your students to trust their intuitive sensibilities.

Those who enjoy uncertainty and challenge usually give their intuition room to function freely. If they are able to blend their intuitive sense with their rational "check-it-out sense," they have a duet of powerful skills for successful problem solving.

Images are potentially malleable building blocks

for creating larger ideas…

rich vehicles for meaning…

they invite grasping, handling, tinkering and building.

—Chuck Palus, Center for Creative Leadership

Visualizing, Picturing the Concept

"I insist that words are totally absent from my mind when I really think."

—Jacques Hadamard, Mathematician

Picturing what we are thinking about is a natural human act. We all do it, we need to do it to really understand.

Friedrich Kekule, a German chemist, discovered the structure of the benzene ring. He was in a half-sleep state when he saw a snake seize its own tail. Kekule's exact words were:

> *"One of the snakes seized its own tail and the image whirled scornfully before my eyes."*

Thomas West,[11] a writer on computer systems, energy, and visual thinking, suggests that the image dared Kekule to understand without words (whirled scornfully), a haughty challenge implying the superiority of visual understanding. West's point is an insightful one: to come to clarity without words may be superior (or preliminary) to understanding things by naming them. Words are limiting. They are oftentimes inadequate to the task of characterizing wholeness.

Clearly, we need words, and our schooling does a fair job of teaching students to use them well. But where are the visual representations so necessary to understanding? Often I have wished that my first math teachers understood this. I had to wait to find one who did, the one who showed me the pictures at last, so I could understand at the meaning level, not the rote, memorize-the-formulas level.

---

[11]West, Thomas, 1991

Visual teaching strategies are not just the pictures, the portrayals of actual things. They can be the representations of concepts that abstract from experience, ideas that are displayed with line and color and movement and music and sound, graphics that show understandings of relationships, and so on.

Open the nonverbal world to your students and you will open them to essence. You will enhance their ability to get to the core of things. How many students would amaze us with what they know if we offered them the option of displaying what they have learned nonverbally?

Multi-modal representations help us conceptualize. They help us see things as wholes so we can compare them to other things. We can take our own images from past encounters and bring them to the task of comprehending what the experts have discovered. We can compare, we can juxtapose, we can blend.

Thomas Defanti, Professor of Electrical Engineering and Computer Science at the University of Illinois at Chicago, commenting on what computer graphics can do to enhance understanding:

> *"With the advent of computer graphics, researchers can convert entire fields of variables to color images. The information conveyed undergoes a quantitative change because it brings the eye-brain system, with its great patterning recognition capabilities, into play in a way that is impossible with purely numeric data."*

Or Thomas West's advice on helping students with visual learning:

> *"Coming full circle, we may soon begin to see that some of those who are best attuned to absorbing and fully understanding problems of vast complexity may be just the ones who sometimes have had the greatest difficulty at the lower levels of the conventional educational system—those for whom the easy is hard and the hard is easy."*

James Clerk Maxwell, British physicist, and Michael Faraday, the originator of the concept of the invisible electromagnetic field, both had the same characteristic way of reasoning. They relied more on diagrams and geometrical notions than on words and symbols. They both shared "unusually vivid and creative visual imaginations."

Einstein was a great fan of Faraday, and writing a thank you note to a friend who had given him a book about Faraday he remarked on the exclusive mathematical-logical approaches to science so prevalent at the time which he abhorred. "You have given me great joy with the little book...In Faraday's day there did not exist the dull specialization that stares with self-conceit through horn-rimmed glasses and destroys poetry."

A new cross-disciplinary field called scientific visualization has proven to be so powerful in this area that it is the subject of many current periodicals. Some of the fields to which this kind of visual and spatial thinking are being applied include: brain structure, astrophysics, analysis of the stress on certain kinds of materials, and the flow of fluids.[12]

---

[12]West, Thomas, 1991

Work Task

List two new teaching strategies you will try to capitalize on using the techniques of visual learning. Here are some ideas:

In social studies:

> Create an abstract line drawing of an experience of a student in the culture of a new school.

In science:

> Create a movement pattern with ten or more of your fellow students to explain how heat is energy.

In history:

> Use color to describe the attitude of American college students toward the Vietnam War.

> Use sound to explain the feelings of America's small farmers during the Great Depression.

1. _____

_____

2. _____

_____

The Metaphor: A Great Teaching Tool

Metaphor: when one thing is another

Simile: when one thing is compared to another, usually involves "like" or "as"

Thinking in metaphor links big concepts to personal experiences. Thinking in metaphor engages the imagination in ways that go both to the inside of things (their essence) and to the outside of things (their impact in the world).

Using metaphors unlocks the kind of thinking that schools have left dormant. Using metaphors is a powerful way to explore conceptual boundaries. Because the metaphor is a whole within itself, it forces essence thinking, it requires a comprehensive approach on the part of the student. Using metaphors helps students connect fact fragments into meaningful wholes.

Practice with these images for thinking in metaphors:
The first two are done for you.

Be a bridge   ***lead people to a new side***

Be a lantern   ***help light the way***

Be rain

Be a tree

Be a bud

Be a beach

Be a blanket

Be the earth

Be a garden

Be a mountain

Be a circle

The metaphor is the link to the concept. Metaphors make connections from the known to the unknown, from the familiar to the unfamiliar, they embrace the whole, they contain personal and cultural connotations, hosts of images.[13] They are image-directed, rather than recall-directed, and as such are powerful leads to essence.

---

[13]Sanders, Judy and Don, 1984

Use metaphors in your teaching, both to explain and to illustrate. They are filled with richness. They forge the links between subjectivity and expert information.

Metaphors and similes may be simple and elegant, or they may be elaborate and complex. Remember all metaphors are flawed in some way, because they contain a certain slant. The distortion is okay as long as we understand the nature of the slant.

Take a moment and think about an important essence piece in the content you teach, something that is crucial to mastery. Come up with a strategy using metaphor or simile. Try it on your students and you will discover who really understands. For example, "Give me a metaphor for the core idea of the story we just read,"or "What might be a metaphor that would describe the tension in a meeting when something that needs to be said, remains unsaid?"

An important part of my content is...

_____

_____

_____

_____

A metaphor assignment for my students that will help them capture it is...

_____

_____

_____

_____

Share your strategy with a colleague.

Evidence from brain research is clear and persuasive.

Just as the left hemisphere has, over the course of evolution, been selected as the site of linguistic processing in right-handed persons, the right hemisphere proves to be the site most crucial for spatial processing...navigation, the use of maps, visualizing objects. playing chess, the use of space.

—Howard Gardner

Spatial Intelligence: The Other Intelligence

Spatial intelligence is very different from verbal intelligence.

Howard Gardner describes it as "tied fundamentally to the concrete world."[14]

It is a way of looking and understanding that is not just representational, but multidimensional. It is shape and dimension, placing things in fields, discriminating surroundings from forms, conjuring up images that produce likenesses, transforming one thing into another, being sensitive to balance, orienting in space.

It is all of these things, an amalgam of gifts and skills, two- and three-dimensional. At the heart of all of it, a sense of the whole.

It is geometry, rather than algebra. It is round, not linear. It is the ability to relate what is happening to patterns from the past. The hundreds of combinations of body, hand-eye coordination, patterns and situations each of us has experienced come to the fore to serve us in action. It is often simultaneous. Some people have more than others.

There is some evidence that music training produces long-term improvements in math and science. The content of these subjects draws heavily on spatial reasoning, on maintaining and transforming mental images. It has been proposed that "the enhanced ability to evolve temporal sequences of spatial patterns, the result of music training, will lead to an enhanced conceptual mastery of proportional reasoning."[15]

Imagine that your geometry students might profit from a fine music program! How do you add spatial intelligence enhancing techniques in your classes? What if you asked your students to illustrate their essays spatially (circles inside circles, arrows, lines flowing into one another, lines in conflict, or intersecting, or parallel)? Or ask them to create three-dimensional renditions of problems, or math functions, or simple systems.

Do you think that would give them some new and interesting insights?

[14]Gardner, Howard, 1993
[15]Rauscher, Frances et al, 1997

How else could you capitalize on thought processes that engage spatial intelligence?

Some examples might be:

- using cuisinare rods to learn place value concept,
- building and manipulating models,
- representing ideas in relationship to one another through spatial drawings,
- manipulating the various elements of a problem in three-dimensional space, or
- even simple mindmaps.

We have insisted

that all students, above all,

be able to express their convictions with clarity and coherence,

to integrate ideas,

and to listen with empathic understanding.

—Ernest Boyer

Language: the Universal Symbolism
for Structuring Experience

The language we speak can never fully contain the wholeness of our experience. "It is always reductionist, always less than the experience it is meant to represent."[16]

The act of creating letter symbols that become words is an act of creating order, attempting to penetrate experience, to grasp it by describing it. Language frees us from the direct experience moment. Language lets us stand aside to examine and name what we have experienced.

The brain perceives, examines the percept, images, and creates the language, the symbols that order the work, that bring clarity. It is what humans do. But teachers must understand the limitations of language.

Our mother tongue gives us a specific view of reality. "Different languages create entirely different maps of reality, different ways of being human."[17]

Western languages with their subject-verb-object structure are sequential, linear, left mode. The language we speak biases us, predisposes us towards some things and away from others.

The more we abstract to create order via language, the further away from the original unity, the center, we get. The more we move from 12 o'clock to 6 o'clock, the more we limit what we have lived.

---

[16]Cook-Greuter, Susanne, 1999

[17]Cook-Greuter, Ibid

Language is not neutral. Meaning is an interpretation. It creates the very reality we are trying to explain, overlaying it with our unique way of seeing.

Teachers need to understand the negatives of applying words and classifications. Students need to know both the potential and the limitations of language, especially verbal language.

We abstract experience by naming it. Language moves learners away from the wholeness of their own experience. Assisting students in becoming more aware of the inadequacies of words will help them to sense the poverty of many of the names we impose on things and each other.

"Every naming requires a new naming."[18]

The work of Susanne Cook-Greuter on Comprehensive Language Awareness is insightful and a great admonition to teachers in this regard:

"Individuals can realize that language is important, but only a partial aspect of meaning-making. As long as they continuously deconstruct and reconstruct their relationship to the phenomenon, they can loosen its grip—they can have language, rather than be had by it...Such a reconstructive frame of mind gives vitality by rending every new veil that comes into awareness, experiencing closure and fixed boundaries as deadly."

[18]Freire, Paulo, 1970

There are multiple ways in which the world can be known...

knowledge is made, not simply discovered...

the forms through which humans represent their conceptions of the world have a major influence on what they are able to say about it.

–Elliot Eisner

More and more living beings discover what it is to make a shape,

an image, to devise a metaphor, to tell a tale–

for the sake of finding their own openings...

to feel oneself in a place where there are always the possibilities of clearings, of new openings.

This is what we hope to communicate to the young,

if we want to awaken them to their lived situations,

enable them to make sense, to name their worlds.

—Maxine Greene

Use Both Processing Modes

Our brains need naming tasks that incorporate right-mode and left-mode techniques. Give your students multiple ways to represent what they are learning. Help them to be multilingual. In the hands of artists, words are not limiting. While enlightening your students as to the limits of language, be sure they understand its profound potential as well.

Introduce them to the wizards of imagery, whose artistry captures wholeness with words, like William Wordsworth, A. E. Housman, Robert Frost, Annie Dillard, Jorie Graham, Mary Oliver, David Whyte.

"Daffodils fluttering and dancing in the breeze"
(William Wordsworth)

"About the woodlands I will go,
To see the cherry hung with snow." (A. E. Housman)

"Something there is that doesn't love a wall." (Robert Frost)

"You don't run down the present, pursue it with baited hooks and nets. You wait for it, empty-handed, and you are filled."
(Annie Dillard)

"A crow hung like a cough to a wire above me...
Every bit of wind toying with his hive of black balance."
(Jorie Graham)

"...that life's winners are not the rapacious but the patient;
what triumphs and takes new territory has learned to lie for
centuries in the shadows." (Mary Oliver)

"Inside everyone is a great shout of joy waiting to be born."
(David Whyte)

Bring many kinds of language into your classroom: multiple perspectives, accumulated wisdoms, both left and right modes, with color, sound, movement. Teach your learners how they create the realities they describe by the way they describe them.

How many languages could you use to help them re-present what they are coming to know?

From the standpoint of the child,

the great waste in the school comes

from his inability to utilize the experiences he gets outside the school

in any complete and free way within the school itself;

he is unable to apply in daily life

what he is learning at school.

That is the isolation of the school—

the isolation from life.

—John Dewey

Doing: The Brain and Action

Education is really about how people use knowledge rather than how much they possess.

Acquiring and mastering skills, becoming fluid and flexible in expertise, shaping the nature of difficulties, becoming a good huncher, developing know-how, solving real problems. These are the skills of a developing brain at work.

These are the goals of education and the means by which our brains, in an ever-changing dance with experience, reshape and respond to challenge.

Learning is the dynamic between the individual and the environment. It is moving, doing, involved. It is not passively sitting in a classroom taking notes for school's sake. We are active, we are doers, we act and respond in response to new experiences.

The brain is a complex, adaptive system with interconnections and feedback loops. It extracts salient features from the outside world figuring out what is going on and how to answer, how to respond, how to learn from each experience.

Design your classroom that way. After the practice, make it real. After the skill is in place, use it in real time, with real results.

Transfer of information takes place simultaneously in multiple brain areas through a complex network of nerve strands.

"Information transfer within the brain is not like a train moving from station to station, but more like the spread of a rumor."[19]

If students are to become experts themselves, we need to offer them many concrete experiences that are real world situations, as they move from novice to expert.

---

[19]Restak, Richard, 1994

How many real problems, in real time, do you give your students?

How much drill is only for school's sake?

What should the balance be?

Move into **performance** assessments.

Make it about how they can perform—

    how they use,

    and do,

    and adapt,

    and create for themselves

    what you teach them.

Make performance the goal of every major unit!

Sit down with your students and tell them what they will be able to do, that they cannot do now, when they have completed the designed work.

Can we create schools that value productive idiosyncrasy and that offer students opportunities to follow their bliss?

—Elliot Eisner

See if outcomes matter to them. If they don't, you and your students are not on the same page. Outcomes need to matter to them. Promise them they will be more skilled, more creative, more able to live better lives when they learn what you are about to teach.

Then make it happen.

"I should like to see a pedagogy that empowers students to create, that empowers them to attend and to appreciate.

I should like to see both carried on with a sense of both learner and teacher as seeker, questioner, someone condemned to meaning, and reflecting on the choosing process, turning towards the clearing that might (or might not) lie ahead."

—Maxine Greene

Creating: the Brain Adapting

Creative people are genuine entrepreneurs. They stay open-ended, like the neural structure of the brain. They perform as a result of what they learn.

For them, nothing is in stone.

Research on creativity is about the communication between the hemispheres. Enriched communication, called bisociation, is the key.

The images and patterns generated by the right hemisphere need to be transformed into workable things. They need to be represented in ways that can be used. They need to be verbalized, the details cared for, the structures created (the assets of the left hemisphere).

Brain-compatible learning is whole-brained. The more creative one is, the more the two sides of the brain are in easy communication with each other.

"The synthesizing right mode and the analyzing left mode produce a third mode of thought, the creative."[20]

Greater coherence and interhemispheric communication is the hallmark of creative people. Creative learning matches the brain's learning patterns moving beyond the known to the unknown. Learners do so through original adaptations they make in their own lives.

The integration of both modes, coupled with actually doing the learning, re-presenting (through their own eyes) what they learn, that is what we need to ask of our students.

---

[20]Benson, Frank 1985

To cease to think creatively is but little different from ceasing to live.

—Benjamin Franklin

It takes courage to be creative.
Just as soon as you have a new idea,
you are a minority of one.

—E. Paul Torrance

"We thus move from a simple assertion that one hemisphere carries out one function and the other hemisphere a rival function, to the more sophisticated claim that each hemisphere, or each region within a hemisphere, contributes to a given activity in characteristic ways.

"...When the left hemisphere is aroused, it promotes certain kinds of analytic and linguistic functions. In contrast, stimulation of the right hemisphere brings spatial and holistic functions to the fore."[21]

Howard Gardner, Professor of Cognition at Harvard Graduate School, in a new book, *Intelligence Reframed,* lists the characteristics he has found that predispose people to be creative. Some of his findings include:

> early exposure to other people who are comfortable with taking risks,
>
> an environment that constantly stretches one,
>
> teachers who carefully up the ante,
>
> peers who are willing to experiment and are not deterred by failure, and
>
> sufficient discipline to master a domain.

Creativity is connecting things,
it is curious,
it is hungry and urgent,
and self-discovery is its reward.

What kind of performance tasks are you asking of your students?

How have you formed an environment within your classroom and your content that exposes your students to risk-taking, to stretching, to experimentation and rigor?

How can you improve on it?

---

[21]Gardner, Howard, 1985

The Relationship Between Left and Right Mode (Hemisphericity) and Learning Type: A New Study

In a new study involving 1,171 people, style types were compared to their left- or right-mode processing preference. The population was mainly educators, including administrators. They were given the Learning Type Measure to determine their styles as favoring Type One, Two, Three, or Four, and also given the Hemispheric Mode Indicator (HMI) to survey their left- or right-mode processing penchants.

From these 1,171 scores on the LTM and HMI measures, a statistical analysis was performed to investigate the strength of the relationships between the two variables.

A cross-tabulation table was prepared with two rows, left- and right-mode hemispheric preference, and four columns, Types One, Two, Three, and Four.

We found a statistically significant relationship between the two.

(Chi-Square = 405.7, p < 001.)

Higher proportions of Ones and Fours favor right-mode thinking and higher proportions of Twos and Threes favor left-mode thinking.

N = 1,173

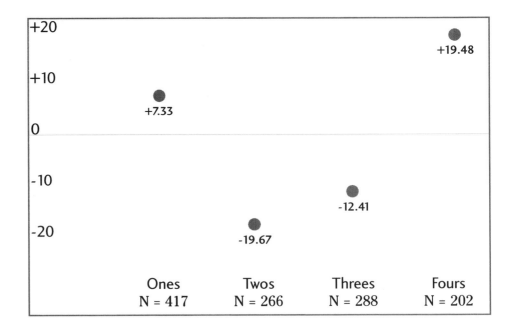

	Ones N = 417	Twos N = 266	Threes N = 288	Fours N = 202

Conclusions from our Research

1. There is a relationship between learning type and left- and right-mode processing.
2. Left- and right-mode processing preference can be considered an element of style.

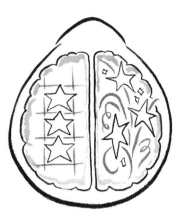

In order to answer the needs of diverse learners in the classroom, teachers need to take style types and preferred brain processing modes in account when they design learning.

Salient Points for Teachers

☆ Every brain is unique.

☆ Learning is driven by emotions, both positive and negative, which are always linked to meaning.

☆ Learning thrives in nurturing relationships which are critical to development.

☆ The brain continually searches for meaning, seeking patterns and personal connections.

☆ People are extraordinarily social, needing to learn in concert with others.

☆ The brain thrives on multisensory experiences.

☆ The brain is a dynamic, evolving manifestation of the totality of our experiences.

Our genes are involved in our learning. Some genes are tranquilized by what goes on in our classrooms. They are bored. A gene wakes up when it learns something. Wake up the sleeping genes. This is how the brain-mind system works.

Think of how desperately important it is to give every child, every learner of any age, as many rich, cognitively rigorous and affectively powerful experiences as possible.

This is the charge for all who aspire to teach.

Chapter Five

The Complete 4MAT Model

Schooling in the United States can and must be revitalized.

This cannot be done, however, by adding an innovation here or there. Systematic conceptualizations of what is required followed by systematic step-by-step reconstruction are called for.

The major educational challenge of our time is to reform our existing schools and school systems.

—John Goodlad

Teaching for Individual Differences and Maximizing Brain-Compatible Learning

The 4MAT cycle begins with being, and moves to thinking.

A lesson unit must begin with being.

It must begin where your students are.

This chapter describes each progressive phase of the 4MAT framework, how to create lessons that move through all four quadrants, and how to alternate teaching techniques with right- and left-mode processing.

The 4MAT cycle requires that teachers establish their conceptual goals, create classroom climates that are conducive to honoring diversity, set up essential questions that go to the heart of the concepts, and create a total learning cycle complete with multiple kinds of assessments.

Quadrant One: Answering the "Why?" Question

You open the learning process in Quadrant One, bounded by the parameters of Direct Experience at 12 o'clock and Reflective Observation at 3 o'clock.

You create a climate of trust and openness.

Oneness: What Your Students Will Experience

☆ Personal, meaning connections based on experience

☆ Sharing storytelling to correlate meaning

☆ Engaging in dialogue (no telling in Quadrant One, please), initiating conversations about the possible meaning of the material

☆ Seeing the material in context to some bigger idea or picture

☆ Establishing relationships

☆ Listening and sharing similar experiences

☆ Speaking with subjective voices

☆ Experiencing camaraderie, having a sense of "having been there too"

☆ Experiencing the diversity of how others see things

☆ Gaining insights into their own experiences through that of others

☆ Creating high interest in the material to come

☆ Establishing resonance

☆ Becoming aware of the value of the learning

☆ Experiencing the discrepancies that the learning will unravel

☆ Focusing on present and past understandings

☆ Creating a sense of "I know something about this, and I want to know more"

The **Climate** is one of trust and openness with permission and encouragement to explore diverse meanings.

The **Method** is discussion of experiences. The students engage in collaborative learning, each contributing their individuality.

The **Teacher** initiates, motivates, and creates experiences that capture the students and strengthens student collaboration.

Dialogue is at the root of the learning process.
—Asa Hilliard

Your teaching task in Quadrant One is to engage students in an experience that will lead them to value and pursue the learning you initiate. Get them to see how the material will connect to their lives.

Learning is not rote, it is how we make meaning. It is directly related to how we feel about what we learn. When we talk about successful learning, we are talking about feeling, answering the "Why?" questions:

"Why do I need to know this?"

"Why is this material valuable in my life?"

"Is there a larger context?"

Answer these questions by making connections with your opening activity.

How would you address the "Why?", for example, in a fifth grade class on fractions? Would your answer be, "Because it is in the fifth grade math book," or "Because it will be on the achievement test," or "Because the state standards say I have to teach fractions in the fifth grade"?

All of those reasons have some validity, but they are not objectives for your students.

Why do children need to learn fractions?

Because they can use them. When they understand that we can look at sections of things in order to comprehend the wholeness of things; when they understand that we can manipulate parts to rearrange wholes; when they understand that some things can be understood discretely, then they will see the importance of "fractionness."

In other words, the content you teach must carry its own "Why?", its own benefit aside from school's reasons. Your students must see the validity of the content for themselves, or you will struggle to keep them focused and attentive.

What is a humanizing relationship?

One that reflects the qualities of kindness,
mercy, consideration, tenderness, love, concern,
compassion, cooperation, responsiveness and friendship.

Education needs to focus on human interaction.

—David and Roger Johnson

Use your content knowledge to create a Quadrant One experience that will lead your students to want to learn, to become fascinated by learning. In the case of fractions, you would set up a situation where they will come to value what fractions are and want to manipulate them for themselves, not for school's sake, not just to do well on an achievement test.

If you do not create a motivational Quadrant One, little learning will follow.

Get your students attention, make your content come alive.

"Attention is the most basic form of love."[1]

Get your students to attend, get them to love the learning!

[1]Tarrant, John, 1998

The kind of learning that should occur stems from the kinds of questions asked.

They should be questions that raise issues, questions that lead to further questions.

Seldom questions are answered with a simple yes or no.

—The Paideia Group

Quadrant Two: Answering the "What?" Question

In Quadrant Two you move learners from experiencing to conceptualizing through reflection, bounded by the parameters of Reflective Observation at 3 o' clock and Abstract Conceptualization at 6 o'clock.

The question you focus on in Quadrant Two is "What?"

> What do my students need to know to master this content?
>
> What are the essence pieces, the core concepts that will lead them to understand more with less?
>
> What parts of this content do I need to emphasize so they will understand it at this core level?

Twoness: What the Students Experience in Quadrant Two

☆ Connecting fascination to facts

☆ Comprehending the learning

☆ Receiving expert knowledge

☆ Examining pertinent information with the most salient facts

☆ Establishing links between subjective experience and objective knowing

☆ Seeing both the big picture and the supporting details

☆ Organizing

☆ Connecting to other similar ideas

☆ Classifying

☆ Comparing

☆ Blending personal experiences with expert knowing

☆ Patterning

☆ Clarifying purpose

☆ Bringing out the structure, the form

☆ Theorizing

☆ Engaging in interactive questioning

☆ Focusing on current hypotheses

☆ Creating knowledge that will give a solid ground to further understanding

The **Climate** is one of receptiveness, taking in, being briefed, a thoughtful, reflective ambiance of attuned and active listening.

The **Method** is information delivery through lecture, readings, and demonstrations to examine expert findings. In Quadrant Two learners cross a bridge from the world of the Self to the world of the experts.

Students bring their experiences in Quadrant One with them to Quadrant Two. Those experiences are processed further **in some nonverbal way** before the content delivery begins.

The **Teacher** creates this bridge with a nonverbal task and then delivers the content, thus melding student experience with expert knowledge.

*We cannot even begin to say
what an intelligence is
until we first ascertain
what kinds of knowledge
are available to it.*

—Jeremy Campbell

For the information delivery part of the cycle, all manner of delivery works: demonstrations, videos, the Web, film, satellite conferencing, etc., anywhere pertinent and current knowledge and information is available.

The teacher moves the learners to objectivity, teaching them to stand aside and examine the concept the way the experts see it, detailing the facts, and discerning the underlying theory. This foundation prepares them for the next step, the mastery of the skills they will need to bring the learning to personal usefulness.

Belief and understanding are not enough.

It has to be done.

—Wayne Dyer

Quadrant Three: Answering the "How?" Question

In this quadrant, bounded by the parameters of Abstract Conceptualization at 6 o'clock and Active Experimentation at 9 o'clock, learners move from expert knowledge into personal skill and usefulness, the beginning of the return back to themselves. The question you focus on in Quadrant Three is "How?"

How will my students use this in their real lives (not just their school lives)?

How will this content affect their power?

Knowledge is the most powerful problem-solving tool there is.

If I want to solve problems in mathematics, I've got to have mathematical concepts.

But there's a difference between teaching knowledge as a tool that facilitates problem solving and teaching it simply as a thing to be memorized.[2]

---

[2]Bransford, John, 1999

Threeness: What Your Students Experience in Quadrant Three

☆ Learning important skills

☆ Practicing

☆ Experimenting

☆ Using expert knowledge to get something done

☆ Testing accuracy

☆ Doing

☆ Establishing the link between theory and application

☆ Seeing how things work

☆ Predicting

☆ Recording the details in action, not just in theory

☆ Questioning

☆ Comparing results

☆ Seeing how form operates

☆ Resolving discrepancies

☆ Reaching conclusions

☆ Mastering skills

☆ Extending the learning into usefulness in real life

The **Climate** is active. Teachers offer opportunities for students to tinker, try things out, to begin to become experts themselves.

The **Method** is working in centers, with partners and in teams (or alone for some students), experimenting, tinkering, practicing.

The **Teacher** is the coach, facilitating, nurturing experiments, guiding the questioning, providing adequate practice for mastery.

The key to Quadrant Three is letting the students discover how valid the learning is **for them.** Require mastery, that they use the learning in their own lives. This is where the learning really starts to take.

Along the path of learning,
playfulness is the thing.

—Unknown

My chief want in life
is someone who
shall make me do
what I can.

—Ralph Waldo Emerson

Teachers who need control seldom go past the 6 o'clock place on the 4MAT cycle. They stay in Quadrant Two where they surround themselves with the safety of the experts. They deliver content, initiate practice routines, and move on to deliver more content. Our textbooks are constructed this way. They prefer to tell and have their students tell back, with little or no change in the telling.

This is not learning!

"Nothing takes root in mind when there is no balance between receiving and doing."[3]

Learning is becoming more—more skillful, more knowledgeable, more skeptical, more capable, more interested in one's own growth.

Learning is never just the test results. It must be used.

Let the material be changed by the student as the students are changed by the material.

Learning is a conversation.

Quadrant Four: Answering the "If?" Question

In this quadrant, bounded by the parameters of Active Experimentation and Direct Experience, learners complete the movement back to themselves.

They refine their use of what they have learned, integrating it into their lives.

The question the teacher focuses on in Quadrant Four is "If?"

If my students master this learning, what will they be able to do they cannot do now?

What power will they have attained as persons?

If they learn this, what new questions will they have?

[3]Dewey, John, 1934

Fourness: What Your Students Experience in Quadrant Four

⭐ Adapting the learning

⭐ Modifying

⭐ Reworking

⭐ Verifying usefulness

⭐ Summarizing

⭐ Creating new questions

⭐ Breaking boundaries

⭐ Synthesizing

⭐ Establishing future use

⭐ Refocusing

⭐ Editing and refining

⭐ Confirming conclusions

⭐ Taking a position

⭐ Creating new discrepancies

⭐ Making new connections

⭐ Evaluating

⭐ Exhibiting, publishing

⭐ Re-presenting

⭐ Performing

⭐ Celebrating

⭐ Sharing the learning

The teacher creates a **Climate** of celebration, one that is performance-oriented, a sharing place with results that can be measured, with new and better questions, with growth.

The **Method** is mentoring, creating resources, and enhancing self-discovery, assisting learners as they adapt and create their own usefulness.

The **Teacher** is the cheerleader, facilitating independence, getting resources, championing, and leading students to meticulous self-evaluation.

The key to Quadrant Four is the adaptation. It is what the learners make of the learning, how they use it in their lives. This is the creative manifestation of the learning. It is the learning activated, behaviorized. It is what Elliot Eisner speaks of when he says learners need to become "idiosyncratic gourmets," putting their individual "spins" on the learning.

Multiple alternative assessments are necessary here to cover the range of unique outcomes inherent in this kind of instruction. Performance assessment requires a specific listing of criteria for evaluation. Students need to know what is expected of them and how they will be measured when they are asked to perform what they are learning, as opposed to merely reiterating what they have been told.

Because each of us is unique, the choices we make to use what we learn lead us back to ourselves. This is how it should be.

Throughout the cycle, the teacher stresses the personal meaning of the learning, first motivating, then informing, then guiding practice, and finally encouraging the imaginative usefulness of performance.

Educators should dedicate their lives to increasing the abilities of their students to master their own destinies.

Keep an eye out
for the tinker shuffle,
the flying of kites,
and kindred sources of surprised amusement.

—Unknown

A Note on the Cycle

If you successfully guide your learners through this cycle, you will have accomplished something very real.

All your students will experience learning.

They will experience comfort, and they will be required to stretch.

Such is all learning, there are places where we are graceful, and places where we stumble.

The stumbling places offer opportunity for growth.

Learners will be drawn into the learning.

They will examine and experiment with significant concepts.

They will integrate the learning into their lives, which will draw them to further learning opportunities.

Through all of it we need to learn how to learn.

And so the cycle repeats, at higher and higher levels.

Work Task
Quadrant One Questions: Establishing the "Why?"

Learning is the making of meaning.

—Kegan

1. Do you introduce your subject by setting up situations learners can recognize, beginning by building on what they already know?

   (5) All the Time   **(4) Quite Often**   **(3) Sometimes**   **(2) A Little**   **(1) Not At All**

   _____   _____   _____   _____   _____

2. Do you set up situations that draw out learners' subjective comments (personal past experiences and feelings) about the material to be learned?

   (5) All the Time   **(4) Quite Often**   **(3) Sometimes**   **(2) A Little**   **(1) Not At All**

   _____   _____   _____   _____   _____

3. How often do you construct actual experiences where your students are involved in some happening, rather than just reading information or asking students to listen to someone give them information?

   (5) All the Time   **(4) Quite Often**   **(3) Sometimes**   **(2) A Little**   **(1) Not At All**

   _____   _____   _____   _____   _____

4. How often do you present a problem that contains within it a hint of the discrepancies that the learning will resolve?

   (5) All the Time   **(4) Quite Often**   **(3) Sometimes**   **(2) A Little**   **(1) Not At All**

   _____   _____   _____   _____   _____

5. How often do you lead your learners into discussions with their fellow students, encouraging them to share personal experiences that will help them understand the value of the learning that is about to take place?

   (5) All the Time   **(4) Quite Often**   **(3) Sometimes**   **(2) A Little**   **(1) Not At All**

   _____   _____   _____   _____   _____

Enter the sum of your responses to the Quadrant One questions.   _____

Work Task
Quadrant Two Questions: Establishing the "What?"

A formal and orderly conception of the whole is rarely present.

—Barnard

1. Do you present the material you teach in broad strokes, determining the key pieces that form the essence, so your students can sense the simplicity underlying the complex?

   (5) All the Time   **(4) Quite Often**   **(3) Sometimes**   **(2) A Little**   **(1) Not At All**

   _____   _____   _____   _____   _____

2. Do you emphasize essential rationales, focusing on understanding and seldom asking for rule memorization?

   (5) All the Time   **(4) Quite Often**   **(3) Sometimes**   **(2) A Little**   **(1) Not At All**

   _____   _____   _____   _____   _____

3. Do you require that learners explore the relationships among various sections of your material?

   (5) All the Time   **(4) Quite Often**   **(3) Sometimes**   **(2) A Little**   **(1) Not At All**

   _____   _____   _____   _____   _____

4. Do you ask your students to synthesize as well as analyze? Do you keep these two in balance?

   (5) All the Time   **(4) Quite Often**   **(3) Sometimes**   **(2) A Little**   **(1) Not At All**

   _____   _____   _____   _____   _____

5. Do you keep returning to the major concepts as you move through the various parts of your instruction?

   (5) All the Time   **(4) Quite Often**   **(3) Sometimes**   **(2) A Little**   **(1) Not At All**

   _____   _____   _____   _____   _____

Enter the sum of your responses to the Quadrant Two questions.   _____

Work Task
Quadrant Three Questions: Establishing the "How?"

If it is not used, it is not learned.

—Luria

1. Do your practice activities emerge from both the main concepts as well as the factual data?

   (5) All the Time   **(4) Quite Often**   **(3) Sometimes**   **(2) A Little**   **(1) Not At All**

   _____   _____   _____   _____   _____

2. Are there elements of play and wonder in the hands-on activities you require?

   (5) All the Time   **(4) Quite Often**   **(3) Sometimes**   **(2) A Little**   **(1) Not At All**

   _____   _____   _____   _____   _____

3. Do you set up opportunities to learn by doing: field-based experiences, information searches beyond the classroom, experiments, and tinkering possibilities?

   (5) All the Time   **(4) Quite Often**   **(3) Sometimes**   **(2) A Little**   **(1) Not At All**

   _____   _____   _____   _____   _____

4. Do you require that your students test or check out the information they are learning?

   (5) All the Time   **(4) Quite Often**   **(3) Sometimes**   **(2) A Little**   **(1) Not At All**

   _____   _____   _____   _____   _____

5. Do you set up situations that call for hunches concerning possible outcomes?

   (5) All the Time   **(4) Quite Often**   **(3) Sometimes**   **(2) A Little**   **(1) Not At All**

   _____   _____   _____   _____   _____

Enter the sum of your responses to the Quadrant Three questions.   _____

Work Task
Quadrant Four Questions: Establishing the "What If?"

The act of creating is the act of the whole person.

—Bruner

1. Do you often discuss the value of making a difference in the world with your students?

   (5) All the Time   **(4) Quite Often**   **(3) Sometimes**   **(2) A Little**   **(1) Not At All**

   _____   _____   _____   _____   _____

2. Do you give multiple options for your learners to prove mastery?

   (5) All the Time   **(4) Quite Often**   **(3) Sometimes**   **(2) A Little**   **(1) Not At All**

   _____   _____   _____   _____   _____

3. Do you engage your learners in open-ended problem solving, where the solutions are multiple?

   (5) All the Time   **(4) Quite Often**   **(3) Sometimes**   **(2) A Little**   **(1) Not At All**

   _____   _____   _____   _____   _____

4. Do you encourage your students to add their own innovations to the requirements of your courses?

   (5) All the Time   **(4) Quite Often**   **(3) Sometimes**   **(2) A Little**   **(1) Not At All**

   _____   _____   _____   _____   _____

5. Do you use rubrics (specified assessment criteria) that are understood and agreed upon up front? Do you ask students to help you construct those rubrics?

   (5) All the Time   **(4) Quite Often**   **(3) Sometimes**   **(2) A Little**   **(1) Not At All**

   _____   _____   _____   _____   _____

Enter the sum of your responses to the Quadrant Four questions. _____

Plot your Quadrant Teaching Score

Directions: Plot the four sums from the previous pages on the diagonal lines inside the quadrant. Then connect the dots to see a picture of your teaching tendencies within the 4MAT quadrants.

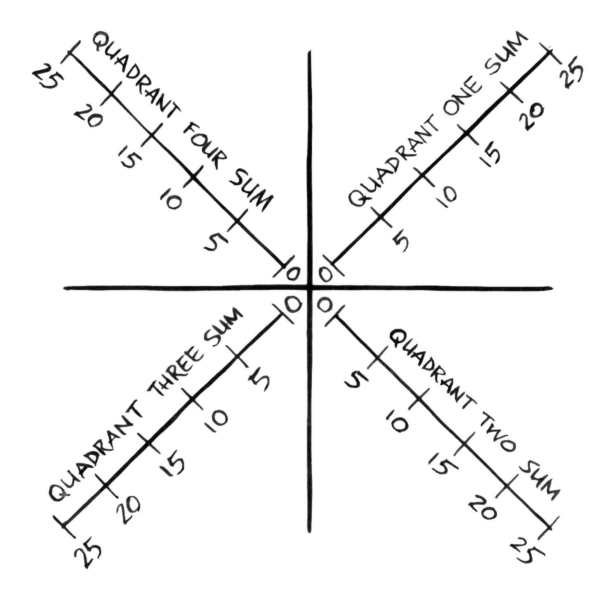

Chapter Five: The Complete 4MAT Model

While we should be wary of simple explanations,
our goal is to render complex phenomena understandable.

—Michael Fullan

Overlaying Right- and Left-Mode to Complete the 4MAT Cycle

The last step in understanding the complete 4MAT model is the overlay of right- and left-mode processing strategies in each of the four quadrants.

The purpose of Quadrant One is to create meaning, to answer the question "Why?"

The right mode is sensory, it comes from feeling. It synthesizes, puts things together. Begin with the right mode.

Step 1: Connect

Establish a relationship between your learners and the content, **connect**ing it to their lives, not telling them how it connects, but having something actually happen in the classroom that will bring them to make the connection themselves. The experience you create must be based on the essence of the content.

Step 2: Attend

Have your students analyze what just happened, have them **attend** to their own experience and to the perceptions of their fellow students; how it went, what really happened.

Allow students to reflect on the experience together, discussing, sharing, seeing similar patterns. After the created experience, have your students examine what just happened, have them step outside the experience, applying the left mode's analyzing skill—standing aside to better understand. If you have established a climate of trust (so necessary for all real learning), your students will become mentors to each other.

As they step outside the experience to discuss it, they will help each other understand the value of the material, the relationships, the discrepancies, and the inherent possibilities.

The Quadrant One Processing Steps are **Connect and Attend.**

Connect: co nectere–to bind with

Attend: ad tendere–to stretch towards

connect

attend

The purpose of Quadrant Two is to inform and enlarge the learner's understanding of the content, to answer the question "What?"

Bring the right mode to bear on the concept under study before you deliver the expert knowledge.

Step 3: Imagine

You need your students to imagine, to picture the concept as they understand it, have experienced it, before you take them to the experts.
(Einstein seeing light curving.)

Right-mode activities such as analogies, metaphors, visuals that capture the conceptual essence (as it is presently known by your students) will bring them to the expert content not as "strangers in a strange land," but as persons who can say, "I already know something about this."

imagine

Step 4: Inform

Students are now ready for the left-mode step of Quadrant Two, receiving and examining the expert knowledge. Inform them of the content they need to understand, give them the expert knowledge.

This is the telling time, a receiving time for your students. This is where a fine, organized, well-delivered lecture belongs—illuminating texts, guest speakers, films, information from Web sources, CDs, etc.

If you do this well, you prepare your students to take the learning away from you and from the experts, and begin to take ownership of it for themselves.

The Quadrant Two Processing Steps are **Imagine and Inform.**

Imagine: imaginen–to create a mental picture

Inform: in forma–to bring form into

inform

The Purpose of Quadrant Three is to practice, to become skilled, to move to mastery, to answer the question "How?"

Step 5: Practice

Stay first with the left mode. Your students must practice the learning as the experts do it. It is not yet time for innovation or adaptation.

They need to learn by practicing. They need to become sufficiently skilled before they can innovate. Think of a musician, practice first, then interpret. Create work practice that is fun, yet demanding.

Facilitate moving through the activities, the centers you create to help them achieve mastery. When a sufficient level of skill has been reached, your students can begin to extend the learning into their lives.

Step 6: Extend

This is where innovation begins. Students know enough, have enough skills to tinker, to see how it works for them, to play with the content, the skills, the materials, the ideas, the wholes and the parts, the details, the data and the big picture, to make something of this learning for themselves, to be interpretive.

The right-mode's ability to see possibilities, patterns, wholeness, roundness is a major asset here. There is no set path, just the processing. Now the various centers in the classroom become very busy. There is no set-in-stone algorithm, just hunches and nuances. There is no sequence, insights arrive as the doing comes together. When this happens in a classroom, it is really something to see.

This is students and teacher engaging in major quality time! Every time I witness it, I am uplifted.

The Quadrant Three Processing Steps are **Practice and Extend.**

Practice: praktikos–capable of being used

Exend: ex tendere–to stretch out of

(Note the step in the cycle opposite this, Attend, to stretch towards. The notion of opposites moves through the entire cycle, a key invitation to growth.)

practice

extend

The Purpose of Quadrant Four is to adapt, to create, to integrate the learning so it can be used by the students in their future, to answer the question "If?"

Step 7: Refine

Again stay with the left mode. The students have proposed an extension of the learning into their lives. They need to evaluate that extension in the cool light of left-mode analysis. Remember the left mode is a stepping back. Other students can critique (students are often the best evaluators of their own work). The teacher suggests, helps with resources, offers. Have them move outside of their own extension, analyzing, improving, refining their work.

refine

Step 8: Perform

Lastly, have your students perform. Look for originality, relevance, new questions, connections to larger ideas, skills that are immediately useful, values confirmed or questioned anew.

Here the students display their understanding, how relevant the content is to them, its connection to larger ideas, how it fits into their world.

Values are confirmed or challenged, knowledge assumes new form. The students are now the true center of the action, the context of the student now embodies the text of the experts.

The Quadrant Four Processing Steps are
Refine and Perform.

Refine: re fin–back again, to limit, to end, to explore the boundary or limit again

Perform: per form–to form through, to shape, to mold, to fashion

(Note the step in the cycle opposite this, Inform, is to add form into. The notion of opposites moves through the entire cycle, a key invitation to growth.)

All real learning leaves us changed.

perform

Chapter Six

Assessment

Looking down the road, it is clear that we simply must devise better ways to measure the full potential of every child.

I surely hope by the year 2000 our assessment procedures acknowledge not just verbal intelligence, but also the aesthetic, spatial, intuitive, and social intelligences in children.

—Ernest Boyer

Introduction:
What Does Assessment Mean?

Assessment is the conversation I have with myself. It is the intrinsic motivation that guides my growth.

It is the conversation that takes place, first, within me as I receive the world, secondly, with others as we share our worlds, thirdly, between my teachers and me as I learn the world of the experts, and finally with myself and my work in the world.

This final conversation, the one I have with myself and my work in the world, is the one that ultimately governs my life.

In order for this conversation to happen (the conversation of my life), I need to listen to my inner voice, the one that knows. This is the voice that most of us ignore throughout our lives instead honoring only the voices of others. Yet if there is a destiny beckoning each of us, who can live it in our stead? Who can act upon this voice if not us?

School culture teaches us that others know better than we. This is true, of course, in some ways. But others do not know, can never know, what it is like to be us, what our hearts and minds and dreams are nurturing, what all of this is coming to be in us.

The healthy human being listens to the inner voice, judging, comparing, and melding it with the outer ones. But ultimately, it is the inner voice that must prevail.

"If judgments of my work are always external, I will be dependent on the judges, not myself. The judgment needs to be internalized. I need to establish the authority of my own voice, to make judgments about my own work."[1]

---
[1]Kallick, Bena, 1991

We need students to come to believe and honor their inner voices. We need to give them permission to speak in their own voices, to have a healthy skepticism about the world, to value their intrinsic sensibilities, while honoring outside voices with earnest care.

We need "a reformulation of assessment, larger conceptions of evaluation for a larger conception of teaching...larger conceptions of evaluation that tell us what is behind the math algorithms, the metaphors, the lines of poetry, the historical periods, the geological ages, and the genetic codes."[2]

What are these larger conceptions of teaching, those that are behind the math, the poetry, the history?

Do your students see relationships that connect for them? Do they deal with content in terms of essential questions, questions that go to the heart, that are contextual, questions that when pondered, discussed, and answered lead to essence? Do they search and find usefulness in the learning? Do they adapt, create, and integrate? Do they gain more power? Do they relate more meaningfully to their world?

Assessment that leads to these things requires the honoring of both the inner and outer voices.

Create assessments that invite the conversation between the inner voice of the Self and the outer voices of the experts. Teach students to trust their own subjectivity while developing their objectivity with expert help.

Honor both voices in your teaching and your students will come to trust both voices for themselves.

---

[2] Perrone, Vito, 1991

Two Kinds of Assessment

On the Way—"How am I doing?" and **At the Gate**— "What have I done?"

There are two kinds of assessment, those that measure what students have accomplished, At the Gate, and those that measure how they are doing, On the Way.

There are a lot of gates securely in place in our schools, but not nearly enough pauses to assess how our students are doing On the Way.

Think of how a music teacher handles both types of assessment. A student is having her third lesson in trumpet playing, the teacher encourages, readjusts, angles the arm level, the fingers...the child is coming along, the measurement is for progress, the teacher is an advocate, a believer in potential.

The student is On the Way.

When, some time later, the student is more accomplished and asks to move up to first chair, a gate has been added, a more precise goal, with more standard criteria. A different kind of assessment.

Why do music and art teachers and coaches understand the difference between these two kinds of assessment and use them so well?

Why is it that "content teachers" use so few On the Way assessments?

At the Gate: To Sum

to measure what was done

quantitative

data for reporting,
making decisions

completion-oriented

What did you learn?

At certain times, "a snapshot"

On the Way: To Form

to perfect a process

qualitative

data for
developing further

developmental

Where are you in the learning?

Ongoing, "a video"

Work Task

Do this exercise with a partner. Review the following list of assessments. Classify each as favoring **On the Way** or **At the Gate** by drawing a line to the right or left from the middle. If you think an "essay," for example, is more At the Gate, then draw a longer line to the left, if more On the Way, draw a longer line to the right.

At the Gate		**On the Way**
Critical performance exit places		*Assessing progress*

A demonstration

A journal

An essay

A term paper

A diorama

A poster

A students-created skit

A mindmap

A group discussion

A quiz

A worksheet

An outline

A three-dimensional model

A unit test

A graph

An oral presentation

A puppet show

Field notes

A metaphor

An interview

If you are going to err in a lack of balance, which error would you prefer?

Too much **At the Gate**, or too much **On the Way**?

Would your answer be different if you were being assessed rather than your students? Share your answers with a colleague.

Did it become clear to you as you did the On the Way, At the Gate exercise with your partner that the answer is simply, "It depends"? It depends on your reason for giving the assignment, where you are in the learning cycle, and how much developmental versus finishing work your students need.

1. Remember that Assessment is the big umbrella. Begin with that idea uppermost.

2. Then list the different assessments you will use, deciding which will be On the Way and which will be At the Gate.

3. Next list the criteria, the rubrics, you will use. You might have an "Exemplary" category; a second less demanding list of criteria for a "Suitable" category; and a third, an incomplete or unsatisfactory category, a "Not Yet" category. (Of course, you may design whatever your version of these categories might be. For example, you might add a "Sufficient" category before "Not Yet," or whatever suits your outcome goals.) Listing the criteria is the rubrics work. Rubrics are lists of expectations for different levels of expertise. Students may choose which list they will aspire to, using the list as a blueprint to achieve their goals. (You also might work with the students to decide what those criteria should be. They are often very good at this.) Your assessments, tests, quizzes, projects, performance requirements, etc., will be measured based on how many criteria the students have met.

4. And your last task will be to assign a grade to that accomplishment.

Assessment: to describe and compare to some criteria

Testing: determining how many of those criteria have been met

Grades: assigning a numerical value to that accomplishment

Assessment: The Process

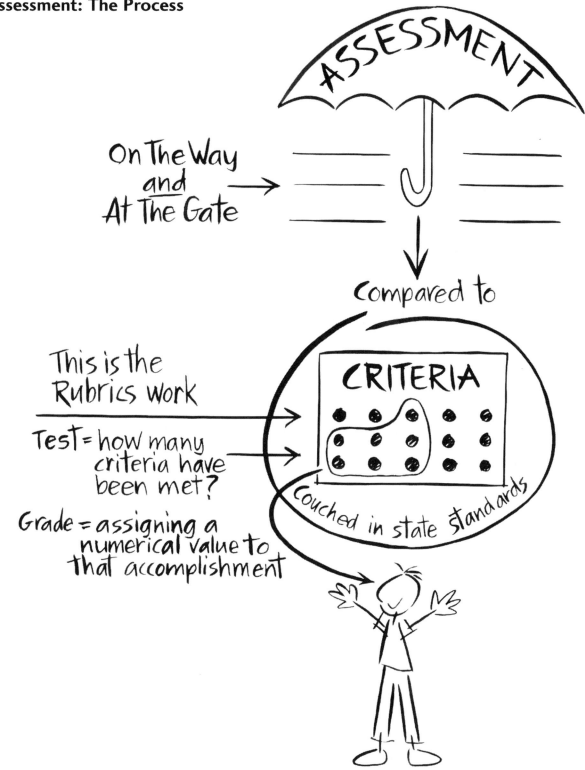

On The Way and At The Gate → ASSESSMENT

Compared to

This is the Rubrics Work

Test = how many criteria have been met?

Grade = assigning a numerical value to that accomplishment

CRITERIA

Couched in state standards

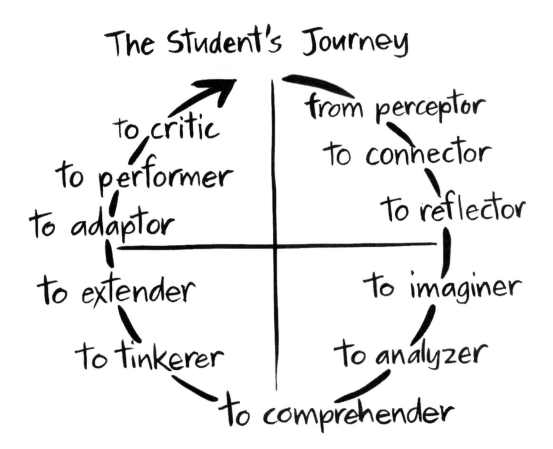

The Student's Journey

from perceptor
to connector
to reflector
to imaginer
to analyzer
to comprehender
to tinkerer
to extender
to adaptor
to performer
to critic

Different kinds of assessment are required as you move around the cycle.

What is the current state of assessment in your classroom regarding these different roles students assume on this learning journey? How many are asked for their perceptions, their connections, to share their reflections, to imagine, to analyze, to comprehend, to tinker with, to extend out into their lives, to adapt what they are learning so it creates something original and personally useful for them, and to become their own critic?

The movement is from perceptor to content receiver to performer. Traditional assessment techniques are not adequate to appraise this kind of journey. The cycle demands alternative kinds of assessments, a wider range of evidence.

Assess the following:

the connections students are making,

Have them draw them, discuss them, give examples of them, "talk story" them.

the comparisons of their perceptions with those of others,

Discuss them, list them singly and then with each other, play with the commonalities found, the patterns in similar personal experiences.

the nonverbal representations of their conceptual understandings,

Creating analogs and metaphors, drawings, three-dimensional illustrations, body movements, i.e., dance or group kinesthetic demonstrations.

the direction of their tinkering,

List their hunches, illustrate their ideas, sequence the steps they have taken, the ones they propose to take, the direction they think they are going, the end results they expect to find.

the way they blend and adapt expert knowledge with their own,

List, write, tell, illustrate expert knowledge along with their own.

their interpretations and creations.

Create performance criteria, be sure the students understand them and act upon them.

The students move from listening to their own voices in dialogue with others, to attending to the voices of the experts, to coming to speak for themselves.

This movement to inner voice is the heart of assessment. Your task as a teacher is to relate your students to the content, to guide them in their journey around the cycle, to lead them to themselves, so they come to speak confidently in their own voices.

VOICES AROUND THE CYCLE

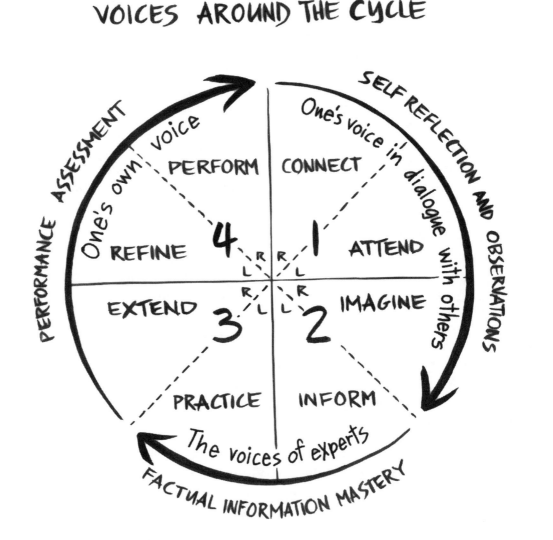

Chapter Six: Assessment

First, the teacher creates an experience, one that **connects** to all the students. Second, students discuss their perceptions, drawing on their backgrounds and particular approaches to experience. This sharing of perceptions leads to expressions of feelings and thoughts about the experience. If the created experience is resonant, the group dialogue will be energetic and authentic.

Students engage each other, **attend** to the learning through personal and group reflection. Assessment here revolves around several issues, how well they attend to each other, their ability to share, their dialogue, and their listing of commonalities, priorities, etc.

In the third step, the Right Mode step of Quadrant Two, students create nonverbal representations of their understanding of the concept, as they have experienced it and pondered it in dialogue with their fellow students. This is the **imagining** step. The key here is the quality of the teacher-created opening experience. It must connect, must be conceptual, must resonate with all the students. If it does, they will be able to attend to it, both in their group dialogue and in their nonverbal representations. The teacher is able to assess the readiness of the students for the information step that follows by examining the students' work from their representations of the concept.

The fourth step is **inform**. This is where learners become receivers. Now they listen. They honor the expert knowledge of those who know expertise in particular content. The teacher delivers that expert content, and makes material available to the students. Assessment here is simply some type of knowledge checking device.

Learning the expert knowledge is not enough. In the fifth step, they need to **practice** what the experts have laid out. While acquiring skills is a concern that is addressed on every step of the cycle, this Quadrant Three, Left Mode step is the primary skill mastery place on the cycle. The teacher assesses levels of skill mastery in this step.

Steps six, seven, and eight are the performance assessment part of the 4MAT cycle. Here the learner finally comes to speak in his own voice. This is the final assessment. And performance is the right word for it.

Step six requires that the learner **extend** the learning into real life. To foster lasting effects on memory and usefulness requires that the students make the material their own. Here teachers need to offer many suggestions, resources, and options. Students may work alone, in pairs, in teams or in centers, and the outcomes for this work need to be rigorously specified. Students can be a great help in writing the criteria, the rubrics.

After the extension is clearly defined and in progress, students move to **refine** their work. This is the left-mode step, the checking things out in the real world. It is an editing phase, an abridging, annotating, revising step.

Finally, the learner adds personal flair and panache and **performs**. The kind of assessments I am speaking of require more diversity in teaching. Performance assessment will never work if students are only given lectures and practice activities. They need to first become engaged in the material so they can form the personal connection. They need to feel the value of the learning, to be drawn to it, and finally, make it their own through some kind of unique adaptation, one that will be behaviored in their lives outside of school.

*Be sympathetic with the type of mind that cuts a poor figure
in examination.
It may be, in the long examination which life sets us,
that it comes out in the end in better shape
than the glib and ready producer,
its passions being deeper,
its purposes more worthy,
its combining power less commonplace,
and its total mental output consequently more important.*

—William James

A Composite of Assessment Around the Cycle

The following pages contain a composite of suggested assessments around the cycle.

The central panel contains the skills we must teach, and the concentric rings move out from the center. The first contains the essential construct of each 4MAT quadrant; the second, the goals for each quadrant; the third, the possible activities a teacher might choose to meet those goals (what the student does); and the outermost circle contains suggested assessments (what the teacher looks for).

Examine the four quadrants of the assessment "racetrack" and the concentric circles.

Note the center of the diagram lists the communication skills which need to be mastered throughout the entire wheel. Each of these skills can be, and should be, used to its highest advantage as your students "travel the cycle."

The "goals" circle has arrows that follow around the entire cycle, as the skills must.

The activities suggested for each quadrant are particularly suited to that quadrant, but not limited to use in only that quadrant. Many techniques can be used in many different ways depending on the teacher's purposes.

What I have listed here make up only possible suggestions. There are many more ways teachers can accomplish the quadrant objectives than are listed here.

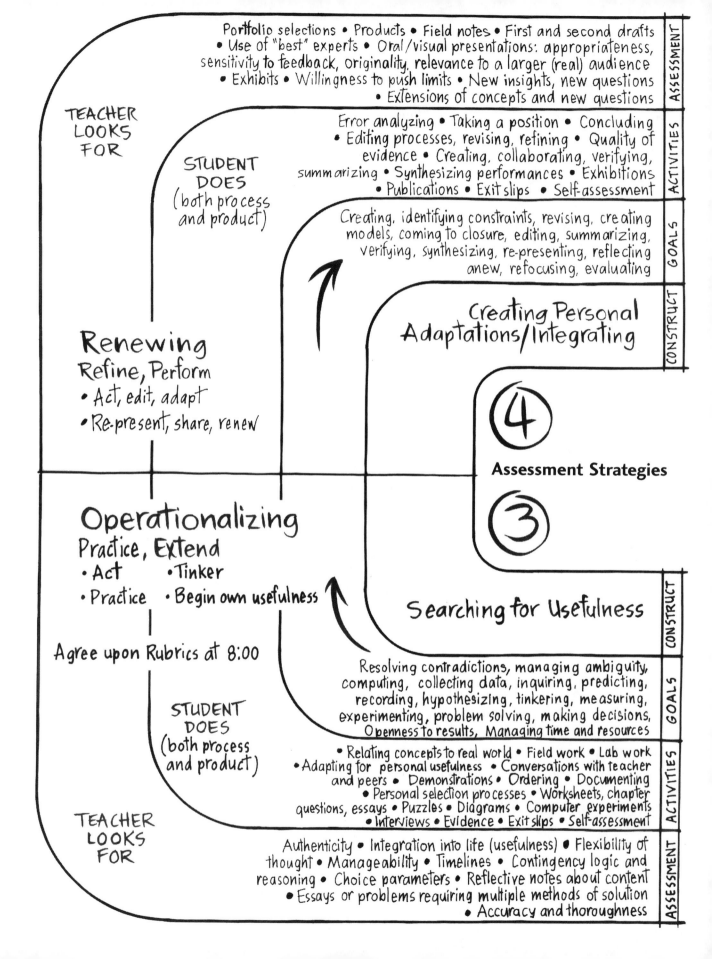

TEACHER LOOKS FOR

ASSESSMENT

Portfolio selections • Products • Field notes • First and second drafts • Use of "best" experts • Oral/visual presentations: appropriateness, sensitivity to feedback, originality, relevance to a larger (real) audience • Exhibits • Willingness to push limits • New insights, new questions • Extensions of concepts and new questions

STUDENT DOES (both process and product)

ACTIVITIES

Error analyzing • Taking a position • Concluding • Editing processes, revising, refining • Quality of evidence • Creating, collaborating, verifying, summarizing • Synthesizing performances • Exhibitions • Publications • Exit slips • Self-assessment

GOALS

Creating, identifying constraints, revising, creating models, coming to closure, editing, summarizing, verifying, synthesizing, re-presenting, reflecting anew, refocusing, evaluating

CONSTRUCT

Creating Personal Adaptations/Integrating

Renewing
Refine, Perform
• Act, edit, adapt
• Re-present, share, renew

④

Assessment Strategies

③

Operationalizing
Practice, Extend
• Act   • Tinker
• Practice   • Begin own usefulness

CONSTRUCT

Searching for Usefulness

Agree upon Rubrics at 8:00

STUDENT DOES (both process and product)

GOALS

Resolving contradictions, managing ambiguity, computing, collecting data, inquiring, predicting, recording, hypothesizing, tinkering, measuring, experimenting, problem solving, making decisions, Openness to results, Managing time and resources

ACTIVITIES

• Relating concepts to real world • Field work • Lab work • Adapting for personal usefulness • Conversations with teacher and peers • Demonstrations • Ordering • Documenting • Personal selection processes • Worksheets, chapter questions, essays • Puzzles • Diagrams • Computer experiments • Interviews • Evidence • Exit slips • Self-assessment

TEACHER LOOKS FOR

ASSESSMENT

Authenticity • Integration into life (usefulness) • Flexibility of thought • Manageability • Timelines • Contingency logic and reasoning • Choice parameters • Reflective notes about content • Essays or problems requiring multiple methods of solution • Accuracy and thoroughness

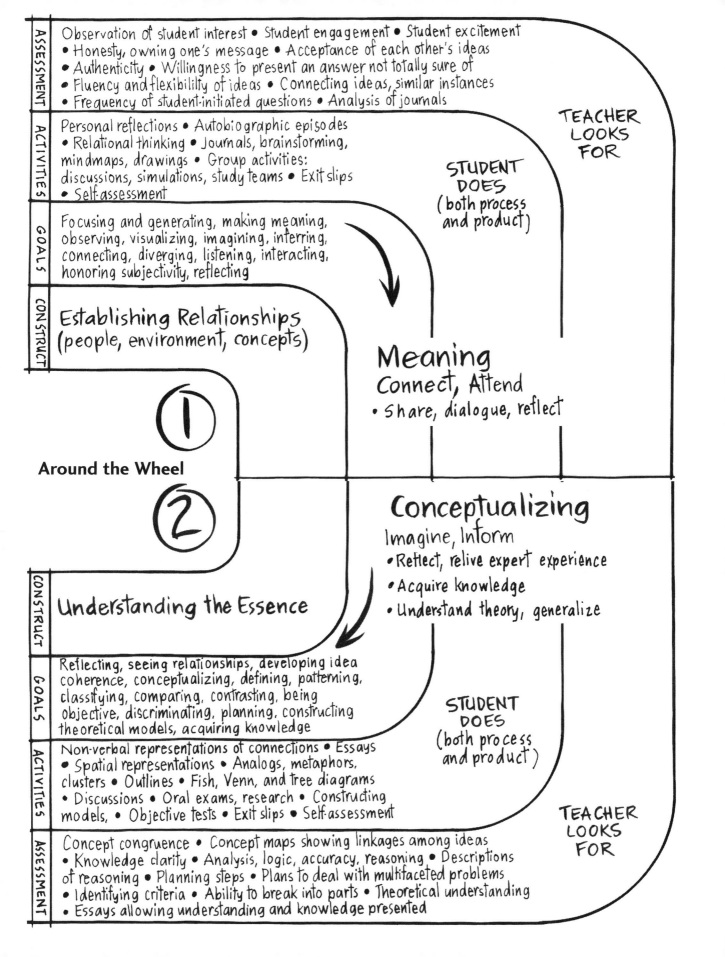

ASSESSMENT	Observation of student interest • Student engagement • Student excitement • Honesty, owning one's message • Acceptance of each other's ideas • Authenticity • Willingness to present an answer not totally sure of • Fluency and flexibility of ideas • Connecting ideas, similar instances • Frequency of student-initiated questions • Analysis of journals
ACTIVITIES	Personal reflections • Autobiographic episodes • Relational thinking • Journals, brainstorming, mindmaps, drawings • Group activities: discussions, simulations, study teams • Exit slips • Self-assessment
GOALS	Focusing and generating, making meaning, observing, visualizing, imagining, inferring, connecting, diverging, listening, interacting, honoring subjectivity, reflecting
CONSTRUCT	Establishing Relationships (people, environment, concepts)

TEACHER LOOKS FOR

STUDENT DOES (both process and product)

Meaning
Connect, Attend
• Share, dialogue, reflect

Around the Wheel

①

②

Conceptualizing
Imagine, Inform
• Reflect, relive expert experience
• Acquire knowledge
• Understand theory, generalize

CONSTRUCT	Understanding the Essence
GOALS	Reflecting, seeing relationships, developing idea coherence, conceptualizing, defining, patterning, classifying, comparing, contrasting, being objective, discriminating, planning, constructing theoretical models, acquiring knowledge
ACTIVITIES	Non-verbal representations of connections • Essays • Spatial representations • Analogs, metaphors, clusters • Outlines • Fish, Venn, and tree diagrams • Discussions • Oral exams, research • Constructing models, • Objective tests • Exit slips • Self-assessment
ASSESSMENT	Concept congruence • Concept maps showing linkages among ideas • Knowledge clarity • Analysis, logic, accuracy, reasoning • Descriptions of reasoning • Planning steps • Plans to deal with multifaceted problems • Identifying criteria • Ability to break into parts • Theoretical understanding • Essays allowing understanding and knowledge presented

STUDENT DOES (both process and product)

TEACHER LOOKS FOR

The purpose of the Quadrant One Construct is to establish relationships between the learner, his or her past and present experiences, and the conceptual connections made from those experiences.

Goals include encouraging students to focus on perceptions, generating ideas to clarify meanings, observing others, and articulating their ways of seeing the world.

Students should also imagine and infer from dialogue, listen carefully with an open mind and heart, attend to and interact with peers, and honor each other's subjectivity.

Activities include personal reflections, stories about autobiographic episodes, thinking relationally, hunching connections, journals, stream of consciousness writing, mindmaps, brainstorming together or alone, collaborative learning activities with partners or in teams, simulations, and studying together with different tasks for each member.

Exit slips that note feelings, new ideas, things to try as a result of this class, and new questions can be jotted down quickly at the end of each learning session and are powerful for both the teacher and the student in terms of monitoring progress.

Assessments might include observing how interested the students are, how engaged, how excited, student ability to be honest, to own their own thoughts and ideas, and attention and willingness to listen to the ideas of others.

How authentic are they? How willing are they to present a partially-formed answer? How avidly do they generate ideas, how do they connect ideas? How often do they ask the important questions?

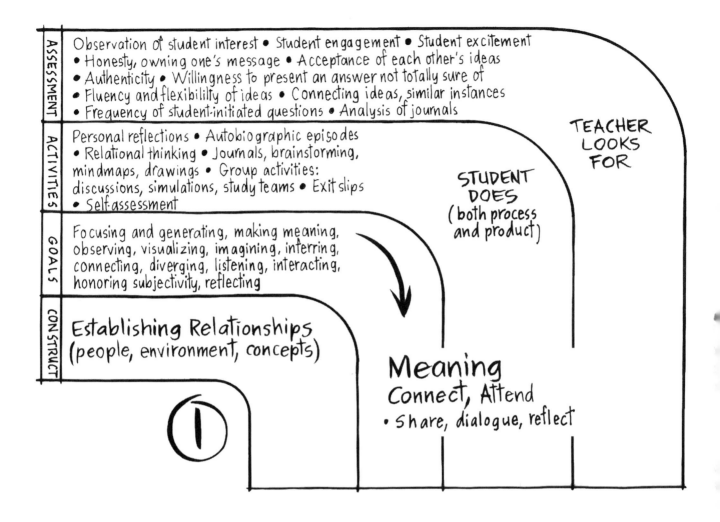

Observation of student interest • Student engagement • Student excitement
• Honesty, owning one's message • Acceptance of each other's ideas
• Authenticity • Willingness to present an answer not totally sure of
• Fluency and flexibility of ideas • Connecting ideas, similar instances
• Frequency of student-initiated questions • Analysis of journals

ACTIVITIES

Personal reflections • Autobiographic episodes
• Relational thinking • Journals, brainstorming,
mindmaps, drawings • Group activities:
discussions, simulations, study teams • Exit slips
• Self-assessment

GOALS

Focusing and generating, making meaning,
observing, visualizing, imagining, inferring,
connecting, diverging, listening, interacting,
honoring subjectivity, reflecting

CONSTRUCT

Establishing Relationships
(people, environment, concepts)

TEACHER
LOOKS
FOR

STUDENT
DOES
(both process
and product)

①

Meaning
Connect, Attend
• Share, dialogue, reflect

Work Task

Jot down a list of the kinds of assessments you regularly give your
students. Compare them to the list of Quadrant One goals above.
Discuss with a colleague.

The purpose of the Quadrant Two Construct is to understand the essence, the core of the content, the big idea that holds everything together and carries the meaning as well as the important details that support and embellish the concept.

Goals include encouraging students to reflect on the images created that illustrate the concept (their own and those of others) and to see the relationships other students see, helping them to form a more comprehensive view of the ideas.

This involves defining, patterning, classifying, comparing, and contrasting the learner's experience with that of the experts. It often involves planning and examining systems. It leads students to objectivity, leaving their subjectivity for a time to examine the material as the experts understand it.

Activities might include nonverbal representations of concepts and conceptual connections, spatially relating those connections, the use of analogs and metaphors and similes, fish, Venn, and tree diagrams, essays, narrative exams, and research.

Assessments might include examining the level of concept congruence between the student's ideas and those of the experts, clarity of understanding of the issues, the quality of analysis and logical reasoning, descriptions of their thinking processes, how well they identify criteria, how theoretically sound their judgments are, and the quality of verbal and nonverbal presentations.

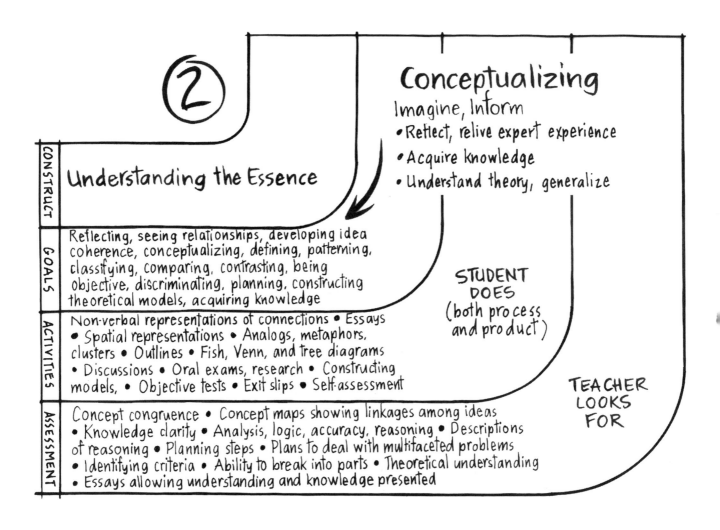

②

Conceptualizing

Imagine, Inform
• Reflect, relive expert experience
• Acquire knowledge
• Understand theory, generalize

Understanding the Essence

CONSTRUCT	
GOALS	Reflecting, seeing relationships, developing idea coherence, conceptualizing, defining, patterning, classifying, comparing, contrasting, being objective, discriminating, planning, constructing theoretical models, acquiring knowledge
ACTIVITIES	Non-verbal representations of connections • Essays • Spatial representations • Analogs, metaphors, clusters • Outlines • Fish, Venn, and tree diagrams • Discussions • Oral exams, research • Constructing models, • Objective tests • Exit slips • Self-assessment
ASSESSMENT	Concept congruence • Concept maps showing linkages among ideas • Knowledge clarity • Analysis, logic, accuracy, reasoning • Descriptions of reasoning • Planning steps • Plans to deal with multifaceted problems • Identifying criteria • Ability to break into parts • Theoretical understanding • Essays allowing understanding and knowledge presented

STUDENT DOES (both process and product)

TEACHER LOOKS FOR

Work Task

Jot down a list of the kinds of assessments you regularly give your students. Compare them to the list of Quadrant Two goals above. Discuss with a colleague.

The Purpose of the Quadrant Three Construct is to make the learning useful, to add to student mastery, both now and into the future.

Goals include encouraging students to resolve contradictions and discrepancies, initiating practice in centers with real-life activities, computing, collecting data, inquiring, predicting, recording, hypothesizing, tinkering, measuring, experimenting, managing time, and problem solving.

Activities might include field work and lab work, learning centers, conversations about results, demonstrations with documentation, worksheets, chapter questions, puzzles, diagrams, computer searches, interviews, lists of evidence, and drills for mastery.

Assessments might include flexibility of thought, contingency logic, quality of choices, met timelines, reflections on process, results reported both verbally and nonverbally, accuracy, the integration of the learning into the student's life and expertise of accomplishment, and what students add to the ideas under study.

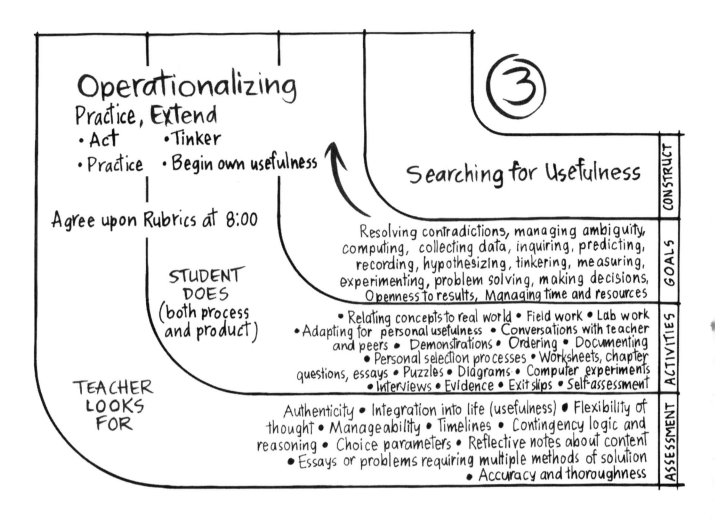

Operationalizing
Practice, Extend
- Act
- Practice
- Tinker
- Begin own usefulness

Agree upon Rubrics at 8:00

STUDENT DOES
(both process and product)

TEACHER LOOKS FOR

③

Searching for Usefulness

CONSTRUCT

GOALS

Resolving contradictions, managing ambiguity, computing, collecting data, inquiring, predicting, recording, hypothesizing, tinkering, measuring, experimenting, problem solving, making decisions, Openness to results, Managing time and resources

ACTIVITIES

• Relating concepts to real world • Field work • Lab work • Adapting for personal usefulness • Conversations with teacher and peers • Demonstrations • Ordering • Documenting • Personal selection processes • Worksheets, chapter questions, essays • Puzzles • Diagrams • Computer experiments • Interviews • Evidence • Exit slips • Self-assessment

ASSESSMENT

Authenticity • Integration into life (usefulness) • Flexibility of thought • Manageability • Timelines • Contingency logic and reasoning • Choice parameters • Reflective notes about content • Essays or problems requiring multiple methods of solution • Accuracy and thoroughness

Work Task

Jot down a list of the kinds of assessments you regularly give your students. Compare them to the list of Quadrant Three goals above. Discuss with a colleague.

The Purpose of the Quadrant Four Construct is the creation of personal adaptations, the integration of the learning into the student's life, the performing of what has been learned.

Goals include synthesizing, re-presenting the learning with a personal "spin," identifying usefulness, revising, editing, summarizing, verifying, and coming to closure.

Activities include analyzing errors, writing position papers, using evidence to demonstrate, exhibiting, publishing, performing, asking better questions, drawing conclusions and backing them up, finding proofs, using art forms to illustrate key ideas, deciding what further study is warranted.

Assessments include products (books, CDs, videos, original drama, artwork, music, scientific findings and artifacts), field notes, first and second drafts, knowledge and use of the important experts, originality, willingness to push limits, new insights, extensions of concepts, relevance to the targeted audience, impact on the targeted audience, and reactions to feedback.

Remember to ask, "What would you do differently?" and "What did you learn that I did not ask you about?"

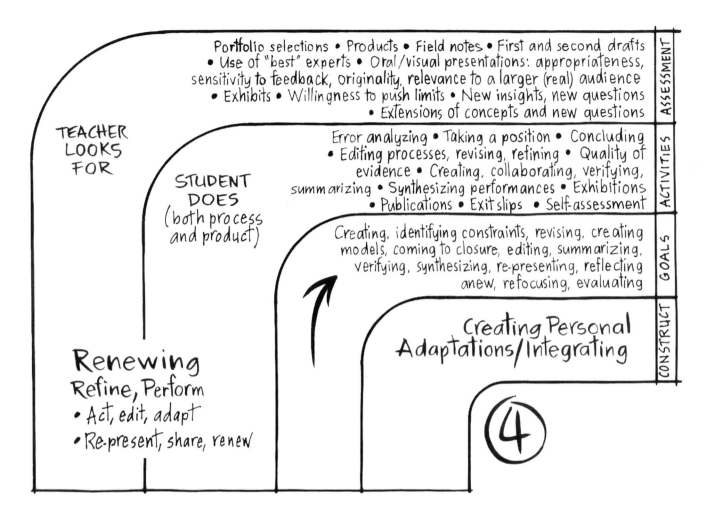

TEACHER LOOKS FOR

Portfolio selections • Products • Field notes • First and second drafts • Use of "best" experts • Oral/visual presentations: appropriateness, sensitivity to feedback, originality, relevance to a larger (real) audience • Exhibits • Willingness to push limits • New insights, new questions • Extensions of concepts and new questions

STUDENT DOES (both process and product)

Error analyzing • Taking a position • Concluding • Editing processes, revising, refining • Quality of evidence • Creating, collaborating, verifying, summarizing • Synthesizing performances • Exhibitions • Publications • Exit slips • Self-assessment

Creating, identifying constraints, revising, creating models, coming to closure, editing, summarizing, verifying, synthesizing, re-presenting, reflecting anew, refocusing, evaluating

Creating Personal Adaptations/Integrating

Renewing
Refine, Perform
• Act, edit, adapt
• Re-present, share, renew

④

ASSESSMENT

ACTIVITIES

GOALS

CONSTRUCT

Work Task

Jot down a list of the kinds of assessments you regularly give your students. Compare them to the list of Quadrant Four goals above. Discuss with a colleague.

Criteria for Measuring: Rubrics, Some Points to Consider

You will need a precise, rigorous rubric to evaluate performance.

1. You must be clear about what you want, the task and achievement you expect.

2. The criteria must be obvious and appropriate. Did the students have time, knowledge, and the resources equal to the task?

3. Your standard of excellence should be available in multiple samples. For example, if you teach composition to eighth graders, get A+ papers in composition from the freshman and sophomore high school teachers. Students need to see the excellence ahead of time, not wait to be told what should have been after they have completed the task.

4. Outcomes need to be observable and results-oriented (what I will see you doing if you perform effectively).

5. The rubric should explain the criteria in detail and have a scoring system attached to it. Consider having students co-create these with you.

What is a Killer for Learners?

Secrecy in scoring
and
No models for progress.

Student assessment should improve performance,
not just monitor or audit it,
and testing should only be a small facet of assessment.

When our aim is to measure,
the child is invariably treated as an object.

—Grant Wiggins

---

[3]Wiggins, Grant, 1993
Read Grant's work for a thorough explanation of assessment techniques.

The major defect with most scoring instruments is the lack of descriptive rigor with which the evaluative criteria to be used are described.

Teachers test in order to make better decisions about how to educate. At least, they ought to.

—W. James Popham

The Assessment Recipe

1. Write an assessment package using all four quadrant goals.
2. Include rubrics for all requirements.
3. Decide which assessments are On the Way, and which are At the Gate.
4. Attach a scoring system.
5. Validate your scoring system by collecting exemplary examples of what you are asking of your students.

Will you use a portfolio, a collection of student work?

Yes___ No ___

What kind of portfolio, by unit, by semester, by year?

Unit____ Semester____ Year____

What kinds of selections will you want included?

_____

_____

_____

_____

At the Gate	**On the Way**
_____	_____
_____	_____
_____	_____

Chapter Seven

Putting It All Together:
Writing 4MAT Plans

Anatomy of a 4MAT Unit: The Ideas

The easiest way to begin the 4MAT planning process is to create a mindmap, brainstorming all the possible content you want to cover. A picture will emerge of the relationships that are inherent in the content. Consult your state standards throughout this process and through each phase of creating your plan.

American Lit: An Example

I will use American Literature for high school sophomores to illustrate the phases of designing 4MAT instruction. There are many ways to go about it, many choices that can be made in terms of content, i.e., what key authors will they read, what particular pieces. The text I referenced in this example was a very comprehensive one and included a great variety of work.

Mindmap the Ideas

Central to the content approach was the big idea of "The American Character." I started with a blank piece of paper, no texts, no standards lists, just my thoughts on what would be significant things for my students to know based on my understanding of the content. In other words, I began with the "What?", the Quadrant Two part of the unit. I drew an oval and wrote in "The American Character." I was thinking of my sophomores' interest in who they were as persons, and I felt I could intrigue them into looking at who they are in light of their American heritage.

I then drew another oval off from the center and wrote "Religion." Religion plays an important role in American culture. I grew up in New England and my background in the early works of American Literature included Puritan writings and work from the Transcendentalists. I penciled in "Puritanism" and added the more generic term "New England." I added "Deism" as a contrast to Puritanism as I was beginning to think about the paradox of opposites as a possibility for fascinating my students.

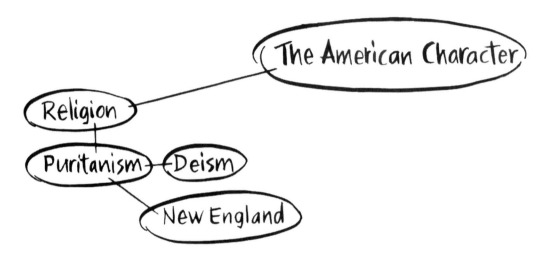

I then changed my direction and began thinking about the creation of the Constitution. I believe the United States Constitution is the ideal human rights document, so I added another oval and wrote in "The Ideal of the Constitution," which led me to "Democracy," which led to "Individualism," which made me think of "The Frontier" and its lawlessness, which led me to add the "Negatives of Competition," which prompted me to think of the positive side of individualism, "Self-Reliance."

Such is how stream of consciousness runs.

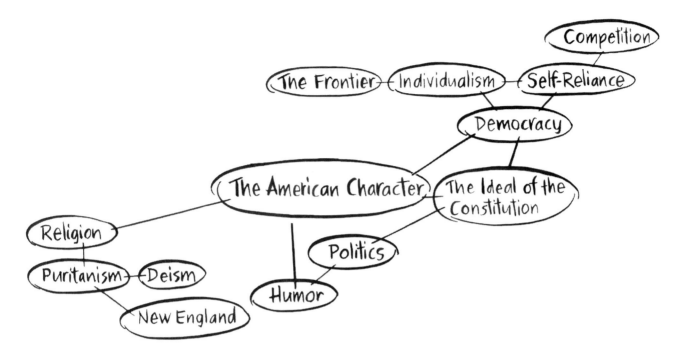

When I looked again at "The Ideal of the Constitution," it made me think of "Politics," which led me to "Humor," which I also connected back to the main concept as I thought about Americans and humor. (I was thinking of a possible contrast of Mark Twain and our present day Mark Russell on public television.)

I decided to leave that set and took another look at what I had so far.

My students were living in a consumer-hungry America. The mall was their hangout place. I worried about their concerns for the larger community, their larger group sensibility. I added another circle and wrote in "The Good Life," with offshoots of "Security," "Freedom," and "Family," the dreams our forebears brought with them when they came here. I then added "The Immigrants" to my mindmap.

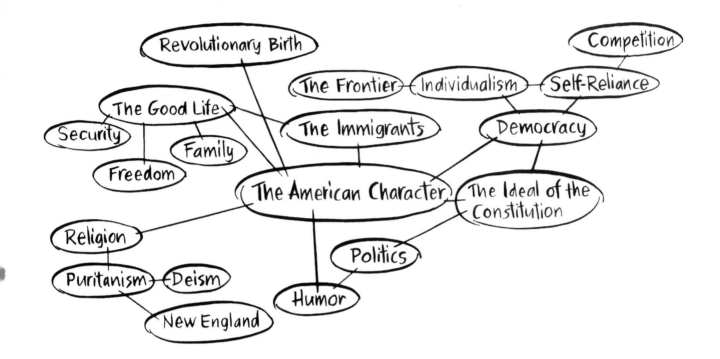

As I looked over what I had, I realized notions of revolution and the revolutionary birth of the United States were missing, so I added them. I scanned the entire mindmap and concluded that I had enough. I remember thinking at that point, "They are only sophomores, and I only have a semester!"

Anatomy of a 4MAT Unit:
How to Determine the Concept

Significant concepts are those that lie at the heart of content. They are the foundation for relationships and intersections with other significant ideas. Our choices depend, to some degree, on the way we see the world. Yet clearly some concepts are more significant than others. We must find and teach the concepts that form the rigor of the content, those that are necessary to understand the structure, those the experts agree are vital to real understanding, that all students must master.

Such concepts are the foundational ideas that encompass the content of a lesson. If the main concept is well chosen, it will help learners realize how the ideas and notions actually function in their lives. Effective concepts are essence pieces, they form bridges, they establish relationships among events, objects, and processes, and, most importantly, they often have immediate relevance for learners.

The difference between a significant concept and a topic is crucial. It is important to understand the difference.

Concept–A significant idea that connects to the main body of content and to the lives of learners.

Topic–A smaller, more discrete section of content that details the elements underlying the concept.

The choices about which ideas are the most important and which form the topical details are yours to make. These choices are based on your own understanding of your content and your knowledge of your students with the assistance of your curriculum, your standards, and your text.

As you brainstorm the content you want to cover, you will begin to see patterns inherent in the material that will lead you to the important ideas, the essence pieces that will tie all the content material together. Look at the relationships in your mindmap. What overarching or "umbrella" concepts might encompass and relate the most important ideas?

Your choice of concepts will form the essence of your instruction. As you travel the 4MAT cycle, it will provide a "home base" for lessons as you:

> set up a climate where students connect their experience to the material,
>
> come to understand it conceptually (conceive the generality of it from personal, specific instances and occurrences),
>
> master it with understanding and skill,
>
> and come to use it in their lives outside of school.

How do teachers come to be conceptually masterful, choosing the most significant concepts and intersecting them with their students' lives? By engaging in this kind of thing. By doing it. Teachers need experience doing it, examining and intuiting the cores of the content, becoming familiar with the expert knowledge. And ideally, doing it together, exchanging ideas and, in some cases, blending two or three disciplines with other teachers. In the American Lit example cited here, history and social studies material is combined with literature.

Finding the Concept

How do you choose your concepts? your topics?

Ask yourself the following questions:

> What ideas form the essence of this content?
>
> What is the structural base of this knowledge or skill?
>
> What are the standards in this content area?
>
> Which ideas will create the strongest connection to my students, which ideas do they encounter every day?
>
> Which will have the greatest impact on their lives?

One helpful exercise we use in our training to improve the ability to conceptualize is what we call the "Movie Exercise." We choose movies that all participants have seen and then ask them, "What is this movie about?" For example, "ET." Our audiences generally proceed to tell us what happened in the movie, giving us a kind of chronological retelling of the events. Then we ask, "What if you could tell us in one word, or just one short phrase, what the movie is about?" To make it easier, we frame it in the following way: ET the movie is a study in what?

What would your answer be? Is ET about relationships? Is it about being a stranger? Is it about overcoming fear with love? Is it about diversity? Which would you choose?

These questions compel us to move from what happened in the movie to what is the core idea of the movie, the conceptualization, the big idea, the whole. We can see the structure, the foundation, the essence through the lens of the big idea.

Some conceptualizations are better than others. Consult your standards, your curriculum, your fellow teachers, your texts, and your own passion about your content.

We become more skilled at conceptualizing the more we do it.

Take another example, a movie most of us have seen, "It's A Wonderful Life." What is the concept of that movie? Is it faith, or good and evil, or rebirth, or something else?

Here are more examples of what we deem effective concepts:

Equations, a study in balance.

The Constitution, a study in democracy.

The Holocaust, a study in dehumanization.

Conflict Resolution, a study in relationships.

Finding the Concept: The Sample from American Lit

In the American Lit example, it seemed to me there was a discernable pattern in the standards that made the major concept choices easier. The cultural background of the United States was formed to a large degree by the influence of religion, individualism, and dreams of the good life. These same three ideas kept appearing in separate standards lists including the content mindmap. I decided that the semester unit would center around these three major concepts. And I would connect them together with the powerful exploration of

"Who Am I?" and "Who Are We, as Americans?", capitalizing on the typical sophomore struggle with identity.

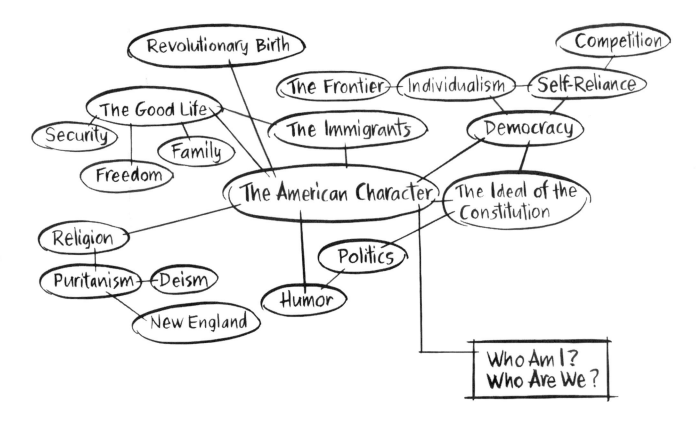

I chose to create three complete 4MAT cycles and teach them in turn: Religion in American Culture, Individualism, and The Good Life.

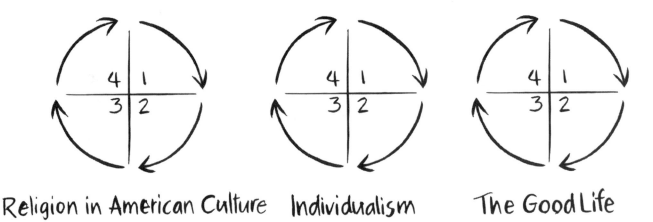

Anatomy of a 4MAT Unit:
The Essential Question, The Next Step

Creating an essential question is a wonderful exercise. It forces you to the heart of the material. You must think through not only the underlying structure, but the very reason you are teaching certain material. The essential question is the core dilemma. It is complex, multifaceted, and most of all, it must be matched to your students and be of real interest to them in their world.

The Essential Question is the glue that holds the unit together. It is the question that learners keep in mind as they work through the cycle. It is the underlying insight. By adding an Essential Question to your unit you will keep learners focused on the core, and keep you, the teacher, focused on the learning outcomes. It changes how learners feel and think. The Essential Question needs to be an important one. Real learning leaves people changed.

Finding the Essential Question

Keep the Concept at the center as you ponder the student's core dilemma. Try framing your unit in terms of the 4MAT cycle.

The major question is "Why? Why do my students need to know this?" As the teacher ponders the value of the learning for her/his students, the essence of Quadrant One becomes more clear.

Then the teacher turns to Quadrant Two, deciding on what part of the content to present (because clearly you cannot present all of any content). This is the "What?" question. How the teacher answers this is at the heart of how the material is conceptualized.

The Quadrant Three question, "How will my students use this in their lives?" and the Quadrant Four question, "If they do, what will they be able to do that they cannot do now?" complete the cycle.

Because the teacher travels the cycle herself as she uses the 4MAT framework, the answers to these four questions often reveal core issues for essential questions. Consider the following examples:

The Constitution, a study in democracy.
Some essential questions might be: How are the rights of minorities kept sacred in democracies where majority rules?

Conflict Resolution, a study in relationships.
How does conflict get resolved if those involved keep the relationship as their key focus, not their individual needs and wants?

Essential Questions and Assessment

The essential question leads directly to outcomes, to achievement goals. What exactly will your students be able to do? The desired outcome will hinge on how well they solve the dilemma of the essential question.

In the democracy example above, some outcomes from pondering the essential question might include: case studies of Supreme Court decisions regarding minority issues, or a debate where the guarantee of individual rights is argued, especially in cases that displease the majority, as in the rights of those who would burn the American flag, for example. So the achievement goal would be an understanding of the tension that always exists between the majority and the minority in a democracy, and how people live within the blessing of that tension.

Anatomy of a 4MAT Unit: The Connection

Next, you must consider Context—the unique environment where learners work and live. Context is vital. Context is what makes it all work. It is not enough to cover well-conceptualized content in an excellent way if it does not connect to learners in their particular time and place. Instruction must intersect with the lives of learners. It must be in their context. The standards, the curriculum, the text, the resources, the logistics, all must be understood in context. Context is the most important contribution teachers make to the delivery of curriculum.

Think "context," how to best connect learners to the content. Try to create an opening strategy that motivates, that gets learners to feel for themselves the value of the material. This is the lesson's opening activity, the first step in Quadrant One, the Right-Mode step. This is one of the most important places in the 4MAT cycle as it sets the tone for the entire lesson and will be revisited throughout. Try to create an experience that will inspire and provoke learners to pursue the chosen knowledge, and to master the skills, one that leads them to value the content. This experience should be imbued with meaning and draw upon previous emotions, experiences, and understandings. It should "hit them where they live."

Remember, the second step of the cycle is the "Attend" step. Begin your units by encouraging learners to voluntarily turn their attention to the ideas being presented. Attention cannot be forced, people are either interested or they're not.

Here are some examples of concepts supported by effective opening activities:

The content is "Romantic Poets," the concept is Rebellion (the teacher presents the romantic poets as the rebels of their time). In the opening activity students bring in examples of the expression of rebellion present in their own cultures.

The content is the "Bill of Rights," the concept is Democracy. In the opening activity, the teacher sets up a totalitarian classroom experience.

The content is "Aerobic and Anaerobic Decay," the concept is Decay. In the opening activity, students "experience" a jar of rotting potatoes.

The content is "Descriptive Language," and the concept is Attributes. The teacher begins by having the learners walk into a classroom strung with clothesline that contains a wild array of old, hippy, tie-dyed, goofy-patterned clothes.

The content is "Scientific Method," and the concept is Problem Solving. The learners are given a mystery box containing one object. They must hypothesize what can and cannot be contained within the box. They are limited to different sensory approaches.

The teacher needs special knowledge of the learners. What will connect to their lives, what has meaning for them? What do they already know that can connect this content for them?

Anatomy of a 4MAT Unit: The Outcomes

List the results you want if the instruction succeeds for the learners.

What will they know and be able to do better?

How will they connect these ideas to their lives?

What will their new skills give them access to?

How will they publicly represent what they learn?

Think about the specific product, performance, and processes that learners will gain from the learning experience. Here, of course, is where the beauty of the Essential Question becomes clear. When learners answer the Essential Question, they are on their way to integrating the learning into their lives. In creating activities that take learners through the cycle, remember the skills the learner will have to discover and enhance. Again, the standards will help maintain the focus.

Anatomy of a 4MAT Unit: The Content

Next, you support your Ideas, Concept, Essential Question, and Connection with specific content and resources. To return to the American Literature example.

The novel for the course was an easy choice. It was *Huck Finn.*

Then short stories were added (these particular sophomores were middling readers and it was decided shorter pieces would pique their interest and perhaps give them more confidence). Steinbeck was added for the immigrant issue, Bret Harte for the flavor of the frontier, Crane for the individualism in *The Open Boat,* with short excerpts from *Red Badge of Courage* and excerpts from Willa Cather for her narratives of the immigrants' dreams of the good life as well as her descriptions of the calamities they endured to make those dreams happen.

The essays and criticisms of Thoreau were chosen for revolutionary spirit and Emerson for *Self-Reliance,* also Thurber and Twain for humor.

Then the poetry: Dickinson and Frost for New England, as well as the work of Edward Taylor to illustrate the Puritan extreme, contrasted with Emerson and the Transcendentalists, Whitman for American individualism, Sandburg for the big city experience of the immigrants, and e.e. cummings for forging new paths.

Next, the music. I chose spirituals and gospel music. I chose cowboy songs for the frontier, railroad songs for the immigrants, as well as *Yankee Doodle* for the revolutionary spirit. I chose the Beatles for "The Good Life" and pieces of blues and jazz to show individualism which is inherent in the improvisational aspect of this music. All of this became the content of the unit. (The music teacher was a great help. Most music teachers would be honored with such a request, and in most cases, you will find they are wonderful resources!)

Anatomy of a 4MAT Unit: The Activities

Next, begin listing the actual activities you will orchestrate in the unit: the experiences, the lecture and readings, the practice pieces, learner performance requirements, etc. Here you begin to work through the 4MAT framework. Consider the entire cycle of learning, including learner motivation, expert knowledge, practice, experimentation, and the creative use of the material.

Specifically:

Construct a learning experience that allows diverse and personal learner responses.

Guide learners to reflection and analysis of the experience.

Use another medium (not reading or writing) to connect learners' personal knowing to the concept, i.e., visual arts, music, movement, etc.

Provide the "acknowledged body of knowledge" using a variety of delivery systems including interactive lecture, text, guest speakers, films, visuals, computer-assisted instruction, demonstrations, etc.

Provide hands-on activities for practice and mastery.

Provide opportunities for learners to design open-ended explorations of the concept.

Help learners analyze their use of the learning for meaning, relevance, and originality.

Make learner creations available to the larger community: the books they create, the information they discover through interviews, their visuals, their demonstrations, the results of their experiments, their illustrated family histories, the scientific findings of local environmental surveys, and so on.

Don't worry about sequence at this point, just consider the above list in terms of the possibilities for making the 4MAT unit come alive! Later, you will overlay these activities on the wheel.

Also, consider the importance of left-mode and right-mode activities. Most units include plenty of left-mode activity usually with less material devoted to the right mode. Add metaphor, visual representations, role-plays, imagery, music, interpretation, feeling statements, peer sharing, subjectivity, etc.

Anatomy of a 4MAT Unit: The Skills

Then take a look at the skills that learners must master as they work through the unit. It helps teachers to create another mindmap of just the skills. Refer to your state standards for more detail: language arts, thinking skills, life skills, hypothesizing, drawing conclusions, and so on. The goal is to marry content and skills using the combination of standards and your own professional understanding of what the task requires to address the diverse needs of your specific learners.

Remember, if the skills are important enough to be included in national and state standards, they are important for all your learners. Design instruction that gives learners the skills necessary to perform the tasks required. This part of the design calls for remediation techniques and alternative ways for learners to master the information in order that all students may master the standards.

Pay particular attention to the skills that are emphasized in each of the four quadrants.

Quadrant One: Focusing, generating ideas, making meaning, observing, visualizing, sharing personal experiences, inferring, connecting, diverging, listening, interacting, honoring subjectivity, reflecting

Quadrant Two: Reflecting, seeing relationships, developing idea coherence, conceptualizing, defining, patterning, classifying, contrasting, being objective, discriminating, planning, constructing theoretical models, acquiring expert knowledge

Quadrant Three: Resolving contradictions, managing ambiguity, computing, collecting data, inquiring, predicting, recording, hypothesizing, tinkering, measuring, experimenting, problem solving, making decisions, practicing

Quadrant Four: Creating, adapting, identifying constraints, revising, adapting models, coming to closure, editing, summarizing, verifying, synthesizing, re-presenting, reflecting anew, refocusing, evaluating, asking new and better questions

While all of these skills are used throughout the cycle, depending on the teacher's intentions, they are particularly useful if emphasized in these quadrants.

Anatomy of a 4MAT Unit: Categorizing Ideas, Content, Activities, and Skills into the Four Quadrants

Now you are ready to create the 4MAT wheel. You can begin to fill in the cycle of activities that will be incorporated in the unit. Spread out all your lists and mindmaps: Ideas, Concepts, Essential Question, Connections, Content, Activities, Skills, Standards, and Outcomes.

Brainstorm all the tasks that learners will do to achieve their goals. How will they come to value the material, to understand it well, to become adept at the skills, and to use it in their lives? Pull the ideas from the content and skills mindmap. There will probably be more activities than necessary. Select the best, and begin to place them into the individual segments of the 4MAT cycle, using your knowledge of the characteristics of each quadrant.

Quadrant One is meaning. Look at the activities list that you created. What jumps out as the experience that will make a connection for your learners? What experience will call on their past feelings and experiences and have meaning for them today? What will bring the value of the content right into the moment? Why does the learner need to know this? What value does it hold for their future? How does this connect to their world?

Quadrant Two is knowledge. What is the best way for learners to become learned in this content? Will it be text, the Web, lectures, films, videos, other people, or some combination? What exactly is the learner to understand? What is the best "expert knowledge"?

Quadrant Three is skills. What are the most important skills in this unit? How does the learner master these ideas and apply them in the real world? How does the learner "add something of himself" to the new material, interpreting, extending? Be sure your learners have the skills they need to do what you are asking. Or be sure to give them the practice and help they need to master those skills.

Quadrant Four is performance. What will learners need to do? What kind of behavior, action, performance are you requiring? Think of the outcomes, and the best ways for learners to achieve them. Think also of options, remember the diverse ways in which students learn and honor them. What will they have a better chance of becoming? What creative manifestations are you looking for?

Right- and Left-Mode Activities: once you've decided where to place the different activities on the wheel, examine them for a balance in right- and left-mode processing.

Left-mode activities are objective, sequential, analytical, and verbally expressive.

Right-mode activities are subjective, synthesizing, metaphorical, and nonverbal.

At this stage, teachers discover they need to add more right-mode activities. We are so accustomed to the verbal, the sequential, that we often forget how much of our thinking is really sensory and intuitive, and how much of what we know cannot be expressed precisely in words. The right mode often functions without words, using images and pictures, discerning the affect, the feeling things, creating metaphors, picking up tones and emotional colors, synthesizing.

We need to ask our students to engage in right-mode processing. We honor their subjective knowing and support their need to express themselves in multiple ways when we build this into our teaching.

Finally, place your chosen activities into the various segments of the wheel.

Anatomy of a 4MAT Unit:
Filling in the Wheel, The Final Step

Fill in the activities that you have chosen to deliver the content, the material you will use in Quadrant Two, Left-Mode **(the inform step)** and Quadrant Three, Left-Mode **(the practice step)** activities.

Then go to Quadrant One, the place where the connection to content is made. Fill in the Quadrant One step **(the connect step)** and then decide how you will have your learners examine what happens **(the attend step)**, how they will analyze the experience, the left-mode step.

Next, go to Quadrant Three, Right-Mode **(the extend step)**. What is the proposed use of the learning? How will learners extend it into their lives? This is a place for options. The activities chosen for this step should provide an opportunity for learners to extend applications into their lives. (At this stage, learners could be in partnership with the teacher planning the rubric, creating the evaluation process together.)

Next, go to Quadrant Four, Left Mode. Here the learner edits and refines his work. This is the critique and edit time **(the refine step)**.

And in the last octant of the 4MAT cycle, Quadrant Four, Right Mode, plan for how learners will share and celebrate the work they have accomplished **(the perform step)**. Hopefully, new questions will arise as a result of the learning. In the ideal, this activity will act as a springboard for the next cycle to follow.

And finally, go to Quadrant Two, Right Mode **(the imagine step)**. This is a difficult step. It is difficult because it should capture not only the core of the conceptualized content, but also the connection between the subjective insights of the learner and the objective aspects of the material. We recommend creating this step last, because it is more apparent then. After looking at the entire cycle, rechecking the Quadrant One connection for congruence with the content of Quadrant Two, and looking again at the unit in terms of learner outcomes, it will become more clear what this activity might be. It should be a metaphorical, nonverbal overview of the connection between the learner and the learning.

Chapter Seven: Putting It All Together

Upon completing this step, go back through the final unit and examine its flow.

Anatomy of a 4MAT Unit: Final Checklist

This book provides a recipe for creating effective instruction. By developing skill in the use of this recipe, it will no longer be a recipe. Rather it will become a kind of buffet, a way to include the essentials of masterful instruction in a manner that suits instruction, the learners, and the content. You will become adept at understanding all the pieces of a complete learning wheel, and will find yourself using them as a repertoire of skills that you can adjust to each unique teaching situation. With 4MAT as a framework, teachers address motivation, they conceptualize content, they teach skills, and they lead learners to performance mastery.

We define a successful 4MAT unit as a cycle of learning. In this cycle, learners...

    have an experience and react to that experience,

    build on experience to examine expert knowledge,

    practice the skills necessary to master the content, and

    become more able, skilled, and knowledgeable as they integrate learning in their lives.

This cycle is an effective framework for high quality learning—one that holds great potential for helping learners make meaningful, useful, and long-lasting connections.

A Further Note About Standards

Teachers need to become familiar with how the experts in their content fields conceptualize their content. One would expect that textbooks would offer this service, that texts would list the significant concepts and there would be agreement among the writers of those texts, and the essence of the content would be couched in ways that are exciting and valuable to students. This is not the case.

Textbooks are disappointing. James Rutherford, Chief Education Officer for the American Association for the Advancement of Science, reports that science texts often have over eight hundred pages of material (supposedly to be taught in one year) with each page containing seven to eight concepts.

"These textbooks often actually impede progress... they emphasize the learning of answers more than the exploration of questions."[1]

To make matters more threatening to teachers, textbook publishers are stuffing as many standard-based elements as possible into their texts in order to get key state adoptions. And because the states do not agree on what comprises the most significant concepts and skills, there is little agreement as to what the most significant concepts are, and the content coverage issue becomes more and more inflated and overblown. So what do most teachers do? They struggle through chapter by chapter, using cursory facts recall assessments that they tack on at the end of chapters.

The Standards

Teachers should be able to access excellent concept lists. There are some lists available to help answer these needs. They are the state standards. In recent times, experts have spent literally thousands of hours debating which are the important concepts and which are the critical skills. Their results are becoming more and more winnowed, more and more elegant. Lists of these concepts and skills are now available. Some are elegant in their simplicity; some are overburdened with trivia. But as content experts struggle to produce these lists, they are becoming more on target and, as such, these lists can become important tools for teachers.

---

[1]Rutherford, James, 1990

Here is how *Science for All Americans* recounts their decision process:

"The recommendations are not those of a single person, nor are they those of a committee...individual panel members had to defend their propositions in terms of both scientific and educational significance. As the number that survived this critical test grew, another condition was added: what should be stricken from the list to make room for the new candidate? The panels had an opportunity to study and criticize recommendations...then the staff, with the experts, prepared a single cogent report...drafts were written, then rewritten. When the Council was finally satisfied, the draft was reviewed in detail by 130 highly qualified persons, their comments studied, and a final draft prepared. The American Association for the Advancement of Science Board of Directors read the entire document, discussed it at length, then voted unanimously to publish."[2]

This is an impressive process, one that creates lists of the best concepts and skills in each content area. Marc Tucker, President of the National Center on Education and the Economy and codirector of the New Standards Project, the nation's largest effort to create a system of performance standards for our schools, says, "Our view is simple. The academic and work-related skills embodied in the New Standards performance standards are the essentials."[3]

Standards are the menus of ideas and skills that teachers match to their particular students. Yet some of the standards lists are better than others. Some states have done a better job. The same is true for the professional organizations, some are more useful than others. The excellence is in the winnowing, where more is less, where the excellence is found in the simplicity. For example, *Science for All Americans* recommends six common themes that should carry throughout the science curriculum: systems, models, constancy, patterns of change, evolution, and scale.

These are workable. Teachers can use these big ideas to construct content relationships that will cover the major, important ideas their students must master. Research shows standards set by individual faculties vary widely in rigor. The reason is variance in expectations. This raises the issue of who should make the final decisions on the standards. Research found that students who

[2]Rutherford, James, 1990
[3]Tucker, Marc and Judy Codding, 1998

scored high on their state assessments scored low on the National Assessment of Educational Progress, a highly regarded survey of benchmark standards.[4]

Individual faculties need to honor the best lists of standards as they create adaptations of them for their own students, holding themselves to more than just local standards. Virtually all standards efforts reference the efforts of content experts who gather together for thousands of hours before making final decisions.

The Best Use of Standards

For educators to avail themselves of the best concepts and skills as delineated by the experts, using them as resources and adapting them to their particular learners, in their particular time and place.

A blueprint for competence for all students enabling teachers to exercise their professional judgement to adapt their teaching strategies to their students' unique needs.

And the amazing irony is that teachers, now already overburdened with texts that go on and on, oftentimes find the standards an additional burden. This is certainly understandable given the variation in quality from discipline to discipline and state to state.

But the standards that have evolved to address themes and concepts rather than thousands of details can be an invaluable resource if teachers pattern and reconceptualize them. So many things have been added to the curriculum without any pruning, it is virtually impossible to know what is essential without this kind of expert assistance.

These content decisions are the guideposts teachers need to manage the vexatious content coverage issue, an issue long overgrown and undernourished.

Teachers need to do the pruning, finding the essence pieces, the ones that will teach more with less. Teachers can turn to their standards for help. Admitting that some lists are better than others, and aware that teachers must deal with what their states require, it is more important than ever to master the technique of conceptualizing content and then connect it to students, using the standards as a resource. Teachers are the primary decision makers in curriculum delivery. They must be the liaison between their students and the standards.

[4]Musick, Mark, 1996

The Right Mix

☆ significant concepts,

☆ aligned with standards,

☆ couched in essential questions,

☆ with performance outcomes based on achievement,

☆ connecting to your students, in their particular place and time.

The successful blending of content and skills to your particular students is the hallmark of master teaching.

Any path is only a path,
and there is no affront to oneself or to others
in dropping it if that is what your heart tells you…

Look at every path closely and deliberately.
Try it as many times as you think necessary.
Then ask yourself, and yourself alone, one question…

Does this path have a heart?
If it does, the path is good;
if it doesn't, it is of no use.

—Carlos Casteneda

Epilogue

In all of this, remember the children.

When a student is bored,
has no heart for learning,
no motivation to grow,
the great gift of inner light is imprisoned,
the light which beholds itself
is hesitant and dim.

We must open a way for that uniqueness,
that glow, to create new clearings,
new possibilities for transformation.

We need to commit our students to meaning.
That is the great task of teaching.
The future of the children,
all the children,
is what we owe to life.

The teacher who moves us to growth,
is the greatest of gifts,
one to be prized above all others.

If, in every classroom,
we had a master teacher,
the world would be transformed.

Bibliography

Aitken, K. J. and C. Trevarthen. *Self-Other Organization in Human Psychological Development.* Development and Psychopathology, 9, 1997.

Abraham, Ralph H. and Christopher D. Shaw. Dynamics—The Geometry of Behavior, Part I: Periodic Behavior. *The Visual Mathematics Library.* Santa Cruz, CA: Aerial, 1984.

Baker, Eva L., Marie Freeman and Serena Clayton. Cognitive Assessment of Subject Matter: Understanding the Marriage of Psychological Theory and Educational Policy in Achievement Testing. CSE Technical Report #317. *UCLA Center for Research on Evaluation, Standards, and Student Testing,* 1990.

Benson, D. Frank and Eran Zaidel, Editors. *The Dual Brain: Hemispheric Specialization in Humans.* New York: The Guilford Press, 1985.

Benson, D. Frank. *The Neurology of Thinking.* New York: Oxford University Press, 1994.

Bogen, Joseph. Mental Duality in the Intact Brain. *Bulletin of Clinical Neurosciences,* Vol. 51, 1986.

Bohm, David. *Wholeness and the Implicate Order.* London, UK: Routledge, 1996.

Bradshaw, John and Norman Nettleton. *Human Cerebral Asymmetry.* Englewood Cliffs, NJ: Prentice-Hall, 1983.

Bransford, John. *How People Learn: Brain, Mind, Experience, and School.* Washington, DC: National Academy Press, 1999.

Bruner, Jerome. *On Knowing: Essays for the Left Hand.* Cambridge, MA: Harvard Univ. Press, 1962, 1979.

Bruner, Jerome. *Toward a Theory of Instruction.* Cambridge, MA: Harvard Univ Press, 1966.

Carroll, Lewis. *The Complete Illustrated Works.* New York: Random House, 1995.

Cook-Greuter, Susanne, R. Comprehensive Language Awareness: A Definition of the phenomenon and a review of its treatment in the post-formal adult development literature. Harvard University Graduate School of Education dissertation, 1999.

Damasio, Antonio. *The Feeling of What Happens: Body and Emotion in the Making of Consciousness.* New York: Harcourt Brace, 1999.

Defanti, Thomas, Maxine Brown and Bruce McCormick. Visualization: Expanding Scientific and Engineering Research Opportunities, *Computer,* Vol. 22, No. 8, 1989.

Dewey, John. How We Think: A Restatement of the Relation of Reflective Thinking to the Educative Process. In J.A. Boydston, Editor. *John Dewey: The Later Works, 1925-1953.* Carbondale: Southern University Press, 1986. Original work published in 1933.

Dewey, John. *Art as Experience.* New York: Perigee Books, 1934.

Dewey, John. *Experience and Education*. New York: MacMillan, 1938.

Diamond, Marian Cleeves. *Enriching Heredity: The Impact of the Environment on the Anatomy of the Brain*. New York: The Free Press, 1988.

Dillard, Annie. *Pilgrim at Tinker Creek*. Cutchogue, NY: Buccaneer Books, 1974.

Dreyfus, Stuart and Hubert. Mind Over Machine: *The Power of Human Intuition and Expertise in the Era of the Computer*. New York: MacMillan, 1985.

Freire, Paulo. *Pedagogy of the Oppressed*. New York: Continuum, 1970.

Frost, Robert. The Figure a Poem Makes. *Complete Poems*. London: Jonathan Cape, 1951.

Gardner, Howard. *The Mind's New Science: A History of the Cognitive Revolution*. New York: Basic Books, 1985.

Gardner, Howard. *Frames of Mind: The Theory of Multiple Intelligences*. New York: Basic Books, 1993.

Gardner, Howard. *Intelligence Reframed*. New York: Basic Books, 1999.

Gazzaniga, Michael S. and Joseph LeDoux. New York: Plenum, 1978.

Gazzaniga, Michael S. *Nature's Mind: The Biological Roots of Thinking, Emotions, Sexuality, Language, and Intelligence*. New York: Basic Books, 1992.

Gleick, James. *Chaos: Making a New Science*. New York: Penguin Books, 1987.

Goldberg, Philip. *The Intuitive Edge: Understanding and Developing Intuition*. Los Angeles: Jeremy Tarcher, Inc., 1983.

Goleman, Daniel. *Emotional Intelligence*. New York: Bantam Books, 1995.

Goodlad, John. *A Place Called School: Prospects for the Future*. New York: McGraw-Hill, 1984.

Gopnik, Alison, Andrew N. Meltzoff, and Patrician K. Kuhl. *The Scientist in the Crib: Minds, Brains, and How Children Learn*. New York: William Morrow, 1999.

Gould, Stephen Jay. *The Mismeasure of Man*. New York: W. W. Norton, 1981, 1996.

Graham, Jorie. *The Errancy: Poems*. Hopewell, NJ: The Ecco Press, 1997.

Greene, Maxine. "Texts and Margins," Arts as Education, M.R Goldberg and A. Phillips, Eds. Cambridge, MA: *Harvard Educational Review*. Reprint Series, number 24, 1992.

Greenspan, Stanley I. with Beryl Lieff Benderly. *The Growth of the Mind and the Endangered Origins of Intelligence*. Reading, MA: Perseus Books, 1997.

Hart, Leslie. *Human Brain, Human Learning*. Oak Creek, AZ: Books for Educators, 1983.

Hayes-Jacob, Heidi. *Interdisciplinary Curriculum: Design and Implementation*. Alexandria, VA: Association for Curriculum Development, 1989.

Healy, Jane. *Your Child's Growing Mind*. New York: Doubleday, 1994.

James, William. *The Will to Believe*. New York: Dover Publications, 1956.

James, William. *Talks to Teachers.* New York: W.W. Norton, 1899, 1958.

Jung, Carl. *Psychological Types.* Princeton, NJ: Princeton University Press, 1976, original, 1923.

Kallick, Bena and Arthur Costa. Through the Lens of a Critical Friend. *Educational Leadership.* Alexandria, VA: Association for Curriculum Development, February, 1991.

Kegan, Robert. *The Evolving Self: Problems and Process in Human Development.* Cambridge, MA: Harvard University Press, 1982.

Kolb, David A. *Experiential Learning: Experience as the Source of Learning and Development.* Englewood Cliffs, NJ: Prentice-Hall, 1983.

LeDoux, Joseph. *The Emotional Brain: the Mysterious Underpinnings of Emotional Life.* New York: Simon and Schuster, 1996.

Lieberman, Marcus. Researcher for the 4MAT Projects. *Responsive Methodology.* Albuquerque, NM. buckml@lobo.net

Lewin, Kurt. *Field Theory in Social Sciences.* New York: Harper and Row, 1951.

Luria, Aleksandr. *Higher Cortical Functions in Man.* 2nd Edition. New York: Basic Books, 1980.

Machado, Luis Alberto. *The Right to be Intelligent.* New York: Pergamon Press, 1980.

McCarthy, Bernice. *About Learning.* Wauconda, IL: About Learning, Inc., 1996.

McCarthy, Bernice and Susan Morris. *4MAT in Action: Lesson Units for All Grades, 4th Edition.* Wauconda, IL: About Learning, Inc., 1999.

McCarthy, Dennis. *4MATION Software.* Wauconda, IL: About Learning, Inc., 1994, 1999, 2000.

McGaugh, James L. Affect, Neuromodulatory Systems, and Memory Storage. *The Handbook of Emotion and Memory: Research and Theory.* Edited by Sven-Ake Christianson. Hillsdale, NJ: Lawrence Erlbaum, 1992.

McGinn, Colin. *The Mysterious Flame: Conscious Minds in a Material World.* New York: Basic Books, 1999.

Musick, Mark. *Setting Education Standards High Enough.* Atlanta, GA: Southern Regional Education Board, 1996.

Noddings, Nel and Paul J. Shore. *Awakening the Inner Eye: Intuition in Education.* New York: Columbia Teachers College Press, 1984.

Oliver, Mary. *Rules for the Dance.* Boston, MA: Houghton-Mifflin, 1998.

Ornstein, Robert. *The Right Mind: Making Sense of the Hemispheres.* New York: Harcourt Brace, 1997.

Perrone, Vito. Toward More Powerful Assessment. *Educational Leadership.* In Expanding Student Assessment. Alexandria, VA: Association for Curriculum Development, 1991.

Piaget, Jean. *Child's Perception of the World.* New York: Basic Books, 1929, Reprint, 1990.

Popham, W. James. *Classroom Assessment: What Teachers Need to Know. 2nd Edition.* Boston, MA: Allyn and Bacon, 1999.

Ramachandran, V.S. and Sandra Blakeslee. *Phantoms in the Brain: Probing the Mysteries of the Human Mind.* New York: William Morrow, 1998.

Rauscher, Frances et al, 1997

Resnick, Lauren. *Education and Learning to Think.* Washington, D.C.: National Research Council, 1987.

Restak, Richard. *The Brain Has a Mind of Its Own: Insights From a Practicing Neurologist.* New York: Harmony Books, 1991.

Restak, Richard. *The Modular Brain.* New York: Simon and Schuster, 1994.

Rutherford, F. James and Andrew Ahlgren. *Science for All Americans.* New York: Oxford University Press, 1990.

Sanders, Judy and Don. *Teaching Creativity Through Metaphor.* New York: Longman, Inc, 1984.

Schacter, Daniel. *Searching for Memory: The Brain, The Mind, and The Past.* New York: Basic Books, 1996.

Senge, Peter M., Art Kliener, Charlotte Roberts, Richard B. Ross, and Bryan J. Smith. *The Fifth Discipline Field Book: Strategies and Tools for Building a Learning Organization.* New York: Doubleday, 1994.

Shlain, Leonard. The Alphabet Versus the Goddess: *The Conflict Between Word and Image.* New York: Viking, 1998.

Siegel, Daniel. *The Developing Mind: Toward a Neurobiology of Interpersonal Experience.* New York: The Guilford Press, 1999.

Storr, Anthony. *Music and the Mind.* New York: The Free Press, 1992.

Tarrant, John. *The Light Inside the Dark: Zen, Soul and the Spiritual Life.* New York: Harper Collins, 1998.

Tenhouten, Warren D. *Cerebral-Lateralization Theory and the Sociology of Knowledge in The Dual Brain.* D. Frank Benson and Eran Zaidel editors. New York: The Guilford Press, 1985.

Tucker, Marc and Judy Codding. *Standards for Our Schools: How to Set Them, Measure Them, and Reach Them.* San Francisco: Jossey-Bass, 1998.

Vygotsky, L.S. *Mind in Society: The Development of Higher Psychological Processes.* Cambridge, MA: Harvard University Press, 1978.

Westcott, Malcolm and Jane Ranzoni. "Correlates of Intuitive Thinking," *Psychological Reports,* 1963.

West, Thomas G. *In the Mind's Eye: Visual Thinkers, Gifted People with Learning Difficulties, Computer Images, and the Ironies of Creativity.* Buffalo, NY: Prometheus Books, 1991.

Whyte, David. *The Heart Aroused; Poetry and the Preservation of the Soul in Corporate America.* New York: Doubleday, 1996.

Wiggins, Grant P. *Assessing Student Performance: Exploring the Purpose and Limits of Testing.* San Francisco, CA: Jossey-Bass, 1993.